STRANGE BEDFELLOWS

STRANGE BEDFELLOWS

Liu Zhenyun

Translated by
Howard Goldblatt and Sylvia Li-chun Lin

CAMBRIA PRESS

Amherst, New York

Copyright 2021 Cambria Press.

All rights reserved.
No part of this publication may be reproduced, stored in or introduced into a retrieval system, or transmitted, in any form, or by any means (electronic, mechanical, photocopying, recording, or otherwise), without the prior permission of the publisher.

Requests for permission should be directed topermissions@cambriapress.com, or mailed to: Cambria Press, 100 Corporate Parkway, Suite 128, Amherst, New York 14226, USA

Front cover image is "Fascination" by Huaisu, cover of *Shanghai Manhua*, issue 8 (June 9, 1928).

Library of Congress Cataloging-in-Publication Data

Names: Liu, Zhenyun, author. | Goldblatt, Howard, 1939- translator. | Lin, Sylvia Li-chun, translator.

Title: Strange bedfellows / Liu Zhenyun ; translated by Howard Goldblatt and Sylvia Li-chun Lin.

Other titles: Chi gua shi dai de er nü men. English

Description: Amherst, New York : Cambria Press, [2021] | Summary: "This intriguing novel-written by one of China's top authors, who has won literary prizes and acclaim internationally-is an important book in China and needs to be known globally. Author Liu Zhenyun's social criticism goes right up to the line that would get him censored or banned in China. The book offers not just criticism of official corruption, but also of China's pervasive new mercenary values, scam artists, and the common folks' vulnerability to scam artists. Hence the novel is not just about China but also a human comedy. This fast-paced but slow-burning farce about the everyday absurdities and challenges of day-to-day existence in China is eloquently delivered in Liu Zhenyun's usual minimalist style and faithfully rendered by the translators"-- Provided by publisher.

Identifiers: LCCN 2021022555 (print) | LCCN 2021022556 (ebook) | ISBN 9781621967026 (paperback) | ISBN 9781621966029 (pdf) | ISBN 9781621966036 (epub)

Subjects: LCGFT: Novels.

Classification: LCC PL2879.C376 C4513 2021 (print) | LCC PL2879.C376 (ebook) | DDC 895.13/52--dc23

LC record available at https://lccn.loc.gov/2021022555

LC ebook record available at https://lccn.loc.gov/2021022556

TABLE OF CONTENTS

Part I: Preface: A Collection of Strangers 1

Chapter 1: Niu Xiaoli 3

Chapter 2: Li Anbang 79

Chapter 3: Everyone You Know 161

Chapter 4: Yang Kaituo 163

Chapter 5: Niu Xiaoli 197

Appendix I 229

Appendix II 233

Part Two: Afterword: Everyone You Know 235

Part Three: Main Story: Foot Bath 237

About the Author 257

About the Translators 259

STRANGE BEDFELLOWS

PART I

PREFACE:
A COLLECTION OF STRANGERS

Chapter 1

Niu Xiaoli

1

Everyone who saw her thought she was worth it: Slanted eyes, the left one slightly larger than the right, though you only noticed that if you looked very carefully. Petite—big women are rare in the southwestern provinces. Niu Xiaoshi, Niu Xiaoli's elder brother, was barely 5'2, and he and the woman would be well-matched out walking because his small stature would go unnoticed. But not so if he were with a big woman. Her only shortcoming was a husky voice that made her sound more masculine than feminine, which was probably why she was so taciturn. When spoken to, she merely smiled; and on those occasions when she had to say something, she would never use two words if one would suffice. Definitely not a chatterbox.

"Your name?"

"Song Caixia."

"Where are you from?"

"X X Province."

(A province in the far southwest.)

"It's a very big province. Which county?"

"Qinhan."

(The questioner was unfamiliar with Qinhan.)

"How many in your family?"

"Seven."

"Who are they?"

"Grandpa, Grandma, Pa, Ma, Big Brother, Kid Sister, and me."

"Why are you marrying someone here?"

"We're poor."

"All this way because you're poor?"

"My pa's sick."

The next question got no response, as tears filled her eyes.

"You must be homesick," the questioner said.

Niu Xiaoli had brought the girl from Old Xin's home in Xin Village. Old Xin's wife was from the woman's province. "She's a niece on my side of the family," she said as she negotiated the price, opening at 150,000 *yuan*. This was not called a sale but rather a betrothal gift, to make it legal. Xiaoli countered with 70,000 yuan, pointing out Song Caixia's husky voice. That infuriated Old Xin's wife, who clapped her hands and replied, "The third son of Lao Gu from Gu Clan Fort married a woman with a harelip from the same province the year before last. Though she'd had it repaired, it was obvious every time she laughed or cried. A hundred and twenty thousand yuan for her. Last year, the second son of Lao Wu from Wu Village got a wife from another southwestern province, a divorced woman with a child, for 110,000. I won't go any lower than 130,000. They need that much for Caixia's father, whose failed kidneys require dialysis three or four times a month. If you don't want her, forget it. But he's in his fifties, my niece is only twenty-one, and a virgin, and I'd hate to see her waste her life as the wife of an old man." Xiaoli continued the negotiations by pointing out the woman's short stature. A stalemate ensued when the numbers were down to 90,000 versus 110,000 yuan. Xiaoli pretended to walk away. Song Caixia stopped her.

"How old?"

The question stumped Xiaoli.

"Who?"

"Your brother."

"Thirty-one."

"And you?"

That too stumped her.

"Twenty-two."

"Are you married?"

"Next month."

"Who else in your family?"

Realizing what Song Caixia was getting at, Xiaoli said:

"Our parents died eight years ago. There's no one at home to make things difficult."

"Your brother is thirty-one ... ..."

Xiaoli figured this line out too.

"He was married but got divorced. He has a four-year-old daughter."

Old Xin's wife clapped her hands.

"You see, I forgot that he's been married and has a child to boot."

"Who wanted the divorce—your brother or his wife?"

That question came as a jolt. Xiaoli gave a straight answer:

"She ran off with another man when he was away on a job."

Song Caixia herself surprised Xiaoli by grabbing her sleeve and saying, "I'll go with you for 100,000 yuan."

Old Xin's wife tried to stop her: "Not enough, don't do it."

Song said that Niu Xiaoli's family alone was worth the extra 10,000 yuan. When Old Xin's wife asked why, Song gave four measured reasons in a soft voice: "First, there are no parents and his sister's getting married next month, so I'll be in charge right off. Second, his wife walked out on him, which means he's mild-tempered. Third, he has a four-year-old daughter, too young to be a problem. Fourth, I don't want to marry a man in his fifties—Old Si from Si Family Stockade." Xiaoli was amazed by what she heard, in part because it was all so sensible, in ways she herself had not considered, which showed that the woman had a good head on her shoulders. More than that, she was already looking into the future, proving that she knew how to get through life. Xiaoli's brother, Xiaoshi, often had no idea what to do about anything, and since Xiaoli was to be married in a month, the house could use someone like the woman.

Xiaoli brought Song Caixia back to Niu Clan Village for her brother to look her over; he did, and so did the neighbors, who crowded into their yard. After the gawkers left, Xiaoli left Song Caixia with a cup of tea and led her brother into the main room to talk it over.

"Well, what do you think?"

"One look won't tell me if there's anything wrong with her."

"In that case, she's the one."

"Can't I have another look? I'm in no hurry."

"I'm getting married next month. There won't be anyone to cook for you and Banjiu."

Banjiu was Niu Xiaoshi's four-year-old daughter. He still had doubts.

"She's got a man's voice."

Xiaoli was losing patience:

"A good voice will cost you 150,000 yuan. Do we have that kind of money?"

Xiaoshi lowered his head and held his tongue—for the moment.

"After all the trouble," he said after a pause, "we end up buying a wife from another province. What will people think?"

"We don't have to go through with it. Go find someone on your own."

Again, Xiaoshi said nothing, this time for a bit longer.

"Let's say we go ahead. A hundred thousand is a lot of money."

Brother and sister had renovated their main room only the year before, and they both knew they were left with only 20,000 yuan.

"Let me worry about that," Xiaoli said.

She went in and told Song Caixia to return to Xin Clan Village and wait till the money was delivered. She then rode her bike into town to see her fiancé, Feng Jinhua. A middle-school classmate of hers, he owned a motorcycle-repair shop.

"Lend me 80,000 yuan," she said.

Feng Jinhua's hands were greasy from working on a motorcycle.

"That's a hell of a lot of money, more than my shop is worth. I make less than 100 yuan from repairing a motorcycle."

"Go borrow it."

"For what?"

"To get my brother a wife."

That caught him by surprise.

"What do I say when they ask me when they'll get repaid?"

"Say when we've got the money."

"When will that be?"

That upset her: "You haven't even borrowed it, and you're already taking their side to make things difficult. Why's that?

"I'll pay it back if he can't, all right? We won't call it a loan, but a wedding present from me. How's that?"

She turned and walked off.

That afternoon, Feng Jinhua rode up to Niu Clan Village on his motorcycle and handed Niu Xiaoli 7,000 yuan.

"I got this from one uncle and two aunts … … when you're in a hurry, you take what's offered. They don't have the kind of money you want lying around."

Xiaoli stared at the little bit of money. "I should have found myself a rich man."

Jinhua's face reddened. "You sprang this on me."

Xiaoli ended the conversation by walking out the door, climbing onto her bicycle, and riding into town to look up the underground banker Tu Xiaorui. Tu's kid sister, Xiaorong, was also one of her middle-school classmates. On one of Xiaoli's visits to her classmate's house, her brother had taken a fancy to her and had then pursued her relentlessly for a good six months. Worried that he looked more like a gangster than a banker, she chose someone else—Feng Jinhua. Feng's appeal was his solid character. Too bad, she discovered a few years later, there's no cash value in character. Tu Xiaorui ran an underground bank under a sign that read "Lanting Teahouse." He was sitting in an old-fashioned armchair staring into space when she walked through the door. She got right to the point:

"Good brother Xiaorui, I need 80,000 yuan."

"I'm in the money business," he said, "and everyone who walks in is God to me. What do you want it for?"

"None of your business."

"Bad news right off the start—three percent compound interest per month for one year."

"But Xiaorong and I were classmates."

"I don't have to charge you interest, but there's a condition."

"What is it?"

"You do it with me."

"Go do it with your sister."

"Okay, a different condition."

"What is it this time?"

"Two percent and you let me kiss you."

She leaned close. As he was kissing her, he held her face in a vice grip and jammed his tongue into her mouth. She pushed him away and spat on the floor. "Fuck you!"

Xiaoli showed up at Old Xin's house that afternoon and handed Song Caixia 100,000 yuan in front of Old Xin's wife. The women went into town, where Xiaoli waited outside the bank while the other two went inside to wire the money to Song's family. After leaving the bank, Old Xin's wife went back to her village and Xiaoli brought Song back to hers. Xiaoshi and Caixia slept in the bridal chamber, while Xiaoli slept with her niece Banjiu.

At breakfast the next morning, Xiaoli saw a furtive smile on her brother's face, and breathed a sigh of relief.

Five days later, her sister-in-law disappeared.

2

Niu Xiaoli had a large mouth, big eyes, a high nose bridge, and was quite tall. She and Xiaoshi were born of the same mother, but he was barely 5'2, while she was 5'9. She was taller than him at age six and still taller than him at twenty-two. From early on, her schoolmates had given her a number of nicknames: Big Mouth, Field Mouse, Elephant, Horsey ... but only behind her back. No one dared use any of them to her face because she wasn't shy about fighting with boys, sending them off with bloody noses with a single punch. So, whenever she heard one of those nicknames, she did not know who they were talking about.

Xiaoli's father died from lung cancer when she was fourteen. Her parents had fought constantly for fourteen long years. She breathed a sigh of relief the day he died during her second year in middle school. One afternoon, two months after that, her physics teacher was telling the class that James Watt had invented the steam engine after seeing a teakettle on the stove judder as steam rose. Xiaoli had a migraine at the time, a condition she'd suffered from since childhood. After asking to be excused, she gave up on Watt, picked up her school bag, and walked home. When she got there, the front gate was shut and bolted from the inside, which she found strange. She climbed the wall and jumped into the yard, where she heard her mother making a racket in the living room. Xiaoli assumed that her mother too was suffering from a migraine, since Xiaoli had inherited the condition from her mother. But when she reached the front door, she heard a man making a whole lot of noise, and she knew what was going on in there. Her migraine went away after she'd stood outside the door for ten minutes, and the shouts inside finally stopped. She kicked the door open, and there on the bed were two naked bodies—man on the bottom, woman on top. She recognized the man as

Zhang Laifu, a cook in town. Her mother was sitting on top of Zhang, who was the father of Xiaoli's classmate, Zhang Dajin; his mother was a janitor at their school. The naked pair were stunned as Xiaoli began to scream, her screams louder than the shouts her mother and Zhang had made moments before. The naked adults were frantic. Without even climbing off the body of Zhang, Xiaoli's alarmed mother cried out:

"Stop that, Xiaoli!"

In an even louder voice, Xiaoli shouted: "Get out of here!"

"Stop that, Xiaoli!" her mother said a second time.

"Father's only been dead two months!" Xiaoli yelled back.

Zhang Dajin's father shoved Xiaoli's mother off him, grabbed his clothes, and ran out the door, pants at half-mast.

"Listen to me, Xiaoli."

"Get out of here!"

Xiaoli's mother froze. "I'm your mother!" she said angrily, "and I'll whip you if you don't stop."

Xiaoli ran into the yard: "If you don't get out of here, I'll shout this out on the street!"

By then, people were leaning over the wall to gawk into the yard.

Xiaoli's mother blurted out: "Wait, Xiaoli."

She dressed hurriedly and ran past her daughter and out through the gate.

"Don't you ever come back. If you do, I'll kill you!"

Her mother never came back, not because she was afraid that Xiaoli would kill her, but because Zhang Dajin's mother learned of the affair, went mad, tossed down her broom at school, picked up a knife, and went looking single-mindedly for Dajin's father and Xiaoli's mother to kill them both. The pair vanished without a trace and were still missing eight years later. Someone said they were spotted at a night market in Xi'an, where they were selling spicy soup and fried flatbreads—Dajin's father was a cook. But in Xiaoli's mind, her mother was just like her father—dead.

Her father was dead and her mother had run off, but she had an older brother, who by rights ought to take care of her. Too bad he was totally worthless. But that was not his fault. His parents had fought from the day he was born. They were arguing when he learned to talk, and they were arguing when he learned to walk—when she was older, Xiaoli concluded that such a background produced two kinds of people. One feared nothing, like Xiaoli, to whom arguing was normal; another type feared everything, like Xiaoshi, who was always picked on in arguments, and thought that was normal. He was married at twenty-six. His wife was a small, phlegmatic woman who never argued, and Xiaoshi did not know how to deal with her because he was always looking for something to argue about. They both had jobs in the city. One day, after an intense argument, she ran off with another man, leaving her daughter behind. After that, Xiaoshi meekly picked up his belongings and took his daughter back to the village. Xiaoli was not upset over his lack of spunk, blaming it instead on their dead father and "dead" mother. With a useless brother and his toddler daughter at home, she had to tend to everything. No longer a kid sister, she assumed the role of a mother. She lamented the fact that she had left school with a migraine that day and gone home, where she'd heard the racket inside. She wished she hadn't kicked the door open and driven her mother away. She should have kept quiet and pretended that nothing had happened. By driving her mother away, she had driven herself into the role of a mother. But she also admired her mother, who had now been gone for eight years without word. That thought led her to understand how a woman who had let her daughter see her naked and straddling a man might hope to be dead to the daughter. This was something she hadn't realized until she had a boyfriend. Once she'd figured this out, she hardly gave her mother another thought. Over time she grew quite comfortable in the role of a mother. She was to be married in a month, and before that happened she needed to find a wife for her brother, which amounted to arranging for another mother for him. On the first night Xiaoshi and Caixia spent together, Xiaoli had slept in an adjacent room with Banjiu. After an hour, she assumed that Banjiu was fast asleep, when the girl said:

"Aunt."

"What?"

"Will they have a baby tomorrow?"

Xiaoli knew that Banjiu meant the couple in the other room.

"No, that takes at least nine months."

"What if my stepmother is mean to me?"

"You've always got me."

"But you'll be married."

"If she's mean to you, you'll come stay with me."

"If I stay with you, what if your man is mean to me?"

Xiaoli was now wide awake. "Screw him. He wouldn't dare!"

Banjiu giggled and put her arms around Xiaoli. "Aunt."

"What?"

"I want to be you when I grow up."

She wrapped her arms around Xiaoli, and once Banjiu was sound asleep, Xiaoli started listening to what was happening in the next room. There was no noise, no conversation, and that worried her. At breakfast the following morning, she saw a furtive smile on her brother's face, which put her mind at ease. She thought that everything was settled and was shocked when, five days later, Song Caixia ran off. She'd tricked them. Back in Xin Clan Village, when Caixia had asked all those questions,

Xiaoli had assumed they were getting a good addition to the family, someone who would assume her burdens. To come up with the money, Xiaoli had let herself be kissed by Tu Xiaorui, who had jammed his tongue into her mouth. Now it looked like the girl with the husky voice at Old Xin's house had seen Niu Xiaoli as an easy mark.

"Fuck you, Song Caixia!" she cursed.

3

Niu Xiaoli and her fiancé Feng Jinhua arrived in Xin Clan Village to confront Old Xin and his wife. Niu Xiaoshi was the injured party, and Xiaoli ought to have taken him along, but a loser like him would have been no help at all, for one thing. Moreover, after his wife ran off, he said something that infuriated his sister. Instead of placing the blame on his wife for what had happened, he began carping at her:

"I told you there was no need to rush into this, but you insisted on going through with it. See what happened?"

Xiaoli wasn't angry over Song Caixia's vanishing act, but her brother's comment rankled:

"I did it to hurt you, okay?"

What Xiaoshi muttered next made his sister even angrier:

"A hundred thousand yuan."

"I borrowed the money, so it's all on me. It's not your problem, okay?"

He stopped there.

Xiaoli and Jinhua rode a motorcycle into Xin Clan Village. Old Xin and his wife were not home. A neighbor told them that they were hauling bricks at a kiln behind the village. A brick factory on the flood plain fired gray bricks out of riverbank sand. After five days in the kiln, the bricks were dunked in water before being carried out. Niu Xiaoshi had worked in the brickyard the previous summer, earning 80 yuan a day carrying bricks. That lasted three days. He returned home not because the work was too hard, but because he could not stand the heat; his back was a mass of blisters. When they came out of the kiln the temperature of the bricks was 60 to 70 degrees, he said. The heat was the same for everyone, but he was the only one whose back was blistered. Utterly worthless, he was too frail for hard work, like a housemaid with the constitution of a wealthy mistress. Xiaoli and Jinhua rode over to the floodplain. She had been there once to bring Xiaoshi a pair of cotton-padded shoes, a necessity during the summer, when the floor of the kiln was 60 to 70 degrees. He had told her over the phone that in the space of a year the flood plain level had dropped significantly from the loss of sand to make bricks. The water level had also dropped as the river surged eastward. They got off to wait at the kiln entrance. Before long they spotted Old Xin and his wife among the brick carriers. They were covered head to toe with brick dust. Steam continued to rise from the water-cooled bricks they were carrying, and from their bodies. Both were very short, and each carried a walking stick. Jinhua walked up and blocked their way.

"Put the bricks down."

Old Xin stopped. He was breathing hard.

"What's wrong?"

"Something terrible has happened."

"What?" Old Xin's wife asked.

"Song Caixia has run off." Xiaoli said.

Old Xin and his wife both sat down hard, spilling the bricks all over the ground.

The four people left the brickyard and sat under a willow tree by the riverbank.

"When did that happen?" asked Old Xin.

"Yesterday morning."

"Could she have gone to market?" his wife offered.

"Not for a day and a night. We looked for her in town and in the county seat. No trace."

Old Xin sucked in a mouthful of air: "So what do we do?"

"That's easy," Feng said. "She's your niece, so bring her back."

Without responding, Old Xin crouched down to light a cigarette.

"But she isn't our niece," his wife said tearfully.

That stopped Xiaoli: "All right, who is she?"

"We don't know."

That really set Xiaoli off: "Then what was she doing at your house?"

"She came looking for me, since I'm from Qinhan, her hometown. She said she was looking to get married, and since she was new to the area, she asked to be my adopted niece, someone she could rely on to find her a good match."

Xiaoli's head nearly exploded with the knowledge that Song Caixia had tricked Old Xin and his wife, just as they'd tricked her. But then she began to question whether they were telling the truth. "I don't care if she's your niece or not. Since I met her at your place, it's up to you to bring her back.

"If you can't do that," she continued, "return 100,000 yuan."

Feng Jinhua: "It's not a hundred thousand. At the interest rate of 3 percent per month, it's 136,000 yuan for the first year."

Old Xin's wife was weeping: "You couldn't sell *me* for that much money."

Old Xin flipped away his cigarette butt and stood up. "So what if you met her at our place? We handed her over to you six days ago, didn't we? She spent five days at your house, didn't she?"

"Yes, she did," Xiaoli replied.

"Well, then, she's a member of your family. Whoever's house she ran away from is responsible. If you want to talk about finding her, we should be asking you to bring her back to us, instead of you coming to us."

Xiaoli and Jinhua were flabbergasted, never imagining that a man that small could have such a devious head on his shoulders. Jinhua went up and grabbed Old Xin by the neck.

"The girl's a swindler, and you're her accomplices. Any more talk like that, and I'll fling you into the river, where you can hoodwink the turtles!

"A couple of brick carriers would never let someone they don't know stay with them," he continued. "Your wife haggled over the price. So, how much of the scam money did you get out of it?"

Jinhua was over six feet tall, Old Xin barely 5'1. If Old Xin had been a bigger man and didn't have to carry bricks day in and day out, he would never have married an out-of-town woman. As Jinhua held Old Xin up like a chicken, his wife ran up and grabbed hold of Feng's legs.

"Good brother, all I did was try to help someone from my hometown. We didn't get anything out of it."

Feng flung her away with a shake of his leg, swung Old Xin around by the neck a couple of times, and hurled him into the river.

"That's what you get for lying!" he snarled.

Spring had arrived, but the water out in the middle was still deep and cold. Old Xin flailed like a drowning chicken and then sank out of sight. When his head surfaced a long moment later, he was coughing and trembling as he struggled to swim to the bank. But as soon as he reached it, Feng picked up the date-wood walking stick Old Xin had used when he carried the load of bricks and hit him with it, sending him back into the river. Six days earlier, when Xiaoli had wanted Jinhua to borrow the money she needed, he'd tried and failed, and she'd called him worthless. But now he showed what he was made of by trying to get Old Xin to come up with the money. Maybe because he'd failed to borrow the money earlier, the loss of 100,000 yuan really bothered him. Old Xin's wife ran up and wrapped her arms around his legs again.

"I'll tell you the truth. We got 3,000 out of the deal. Come home with me, and I'll give it to you."

Feng kicked her away a second time and hit Old Xin again.

"We lose 100,000 yuan, and you want to give us three. How stupid do you think we are?

"You got three thousand out of a 100,000-yuan sale," he continued, "just how stupid were you?"

"It was just a fee for helping," Old Xin's wife said. "If I'm lying, good brother, let Heaven strike me dead."

Xiaoli came up and stopped Jinhua: "Three thousand's enough."

The walking stick in his hand froze in the air.

"What are you saying?"

"Admitting they got money out of it proves they were part of the scheme," said Xiaoli.

She grabbed hold of Old Xin's wife's lapel. "Song Caixia is from your hometown, is that right?"

Old Xin's wife nodded.

"Where did she go?"

Old Xin's wife stammered, "The way things look …… she went home."

"Then 3,000 yuan will be our travel money. Since she went home, that's where we'll go to bring her back."

Old Xin's wife was at a total loss.

So was Old Xin, who stopped flailing in the water.

Niu Xiaoli

4

Niu Xiaoli worked in the town's garment factory, which employed more than four hundred workers in two shifts. The machines never stopped, but the people did. There were a day shift and a night shift, twelve hours each for a monthly salary of 1,800 yuan. Xiaoli did some calculations on her way to the factory to ask for a leave of absence. After working all year, she earned the measly sum of 21,600 yuan. Of the 100,000 yuan she'd given Song Caixia, 20,000 yuan was hers and the remaining 80,000 yuan she'd borrowed from Tu Xiaorui at a high rate of interest. He only demanded 2 percent monthly interest, which she had not told her fiancé. Eighty thousand at that rate would become 99,200 yuan in a year. When you add her twenty thousand, the total for one year would be 101,200 yuan. It would take five years and five months to earn that much without spending any of it to pay for Song Caixia. The figure infuriated Xiaoli:

"Fuck you, Song Caixia!"

To that she added: "Song Caixia, I'll find you and bring you back no matter where you run to."

Xiaoli walked out of the factory after requesting time off and spotted Tu Xiaorui. To the right of the factory entrance was a bathhouse that employed women from the northeast, who drew swarms of clients as if they were flies. In the parking lot in front of the bathhouse, Tu was opening his car door and was about to climb in without spotting Xiaoli. The sight reminded her of the scene when she'd borrowed the money from him and how he'd jammed his tongue into her mouth.

"Good brother Tu," she shouted.

He turned to look. Seeing who it was, he stepped back and, with a look at her and then at the garment factory, he said: "Going to work or just getting off?"

"I want to ask you something," she said.

"What is it?"

She walked up to the car. "You said something to me when you lent me the money the other day. Remember what it was?"

"No, what was it?"

"You wanted to do it with me."

He gave her a long look and nodded.

"Will you forget the 80,000 yuan if I let you do it?"

That stopped him. He gave her another long look. She raised her head to give him a better look. He reached out and touched her head. "You're not sick."

"What does that mean?"

"What I meant at the time was, I'd be willing to forget the interest, but not the principal."

"I'll let you do it ten times."

Tu pointed to the bathhouse. "Doing it with an eighteen-year-old girl from Harbin costs me 200 yuan. You tell me how many times we'd have to do it for 80,000 yuan, plus interest."

"I'm from a good family, she's a whore."

"Good family or not, it's all the same in bed."

Then something occurred to him: "Ten times if you're a virgin isn't a bad deal."

Then he gave her another long look. "How would I know if you're a virgin?"

She sputtered. She'd fallen in love with Feng Jinhua in high school, and they'd had sex at sixteen, so she was no virgin. Maybe Tu said what he said because he knew all about that. The awkward look on her face made him laugh. He got back in his car, slammed the door shut, turned on the ignition, stepped on the gas, and sped away.

Xiaoli watched him drive off: "Fuck you, Tu Xiaorui!"

Following Tu's reasoning, Xiaoli made another calculation based upon the 200 *yuan* a bathhouse girl charged for sex. She owed Tu 99,200 yuan, which worked out to 496 fucks or 496 different girls. If she had let Tu do it with her ten times, one fuck would be worth 9,920 yuan. Strictly in terms of sex, what Tu said made sense. She sighed. If she were still a virgin, doing it ten times with Tu to forgive a debt of 99,200 yuan would cancel the need for her to travel to the southwestern province. In a moment of anger, she'd said, I'll find you and bring you back no matter where you run to. Now that she had calmed down, doubts crept into her head as she thought about a place she'd never been to. But she had no options, so off she'd go.

At home Niu Xiaoshi, Feng Jinhua, and Banjiu looked on as Xiaoli packed her things.

"Forget it," Xiaoshi said, "you don't have to go."

"Will you pay Tu Xiaorui the 108,800 yuan we owe him if I don't?"

Since Feng Jinhua was there, she'd told him the figure for 3 percent interest. Xiaoshi said nothing.

"Forget it," Feng agreed, "don't go. We'll find another way to get the money."

"If you could have thought of another way, I wouldn't have borrowed the money with such high interest in the first place."

Feng said nothing more.

"I'm not going there to find Song Caixia only for the money," she said.

"What else then?"

"I want to ask her a question."

"What's that?"

"I thought she was honest and reliable when we first met her. What was it that made her think I was a dumb fuck?"

"I took her to be an honest person," she continued, "and she was able to trick me by pretending to be one. If I'm not a dumb fuck, what am I?" She broke down and cried.

With a tsk-tsk Feng said: "We're supposed to be married in a month. We've already set the happy date. Will this trip delay that?"

"If I don't fix this outrageous problem," she fumed, "I'm not getting married. How can I ever be happy if I don't?"

Feng said nothing, but Banjiu did: "I want to go with you, Aunt."

"Why?"

"I've never been on a train. I want to ride on one with you."

Xiaoli chuckled at that: "I'm going there to find a sworn enemy, not take a vacation. We'll get you on a train some other time."

"Why don't I go with you?" Feng volunteered. "I can help once you find her."

Xiaoli shook her head: "I won't need anyone but Old Xin's wife. She knows her way around her hometown. I've got something else for you to do here."

"What's that?"

"I don't know a thing about the place. If she tries to pull something on me there, I'll phone you and you'll fling her husband into the river again."

5

Niu Xiaoli and Old Xin's wife agreed to meet at the town's bus station at eight o'clock the next morning; they would travel together to Qinhan County to find Song Caixia. After Old Xin crawled out of the river the day before, Xiaoli and Jinhua accompanied him and his wife to their house in Xin Clan Village. They went there to claim the 3,000 yuan the couple had earned from introducing them to Song. They'd use that for travel expenses. But when they got there, Old Xin told them they'd put the money in the bank six days earlier. It was a fixed deposit account, so they'd have to borrow the 3,000 yuan from a relative. Since it was to be used for travel expenses, Old Xin's wife would bring the money with her when she met Xiaoli the next morning. Feng believed that Old Xin was trying to pull a fast one and would have slugged him if Xiaoli hadn't stopped him and said that if the money wasn't handed over the next day, they'd do more than slug Old Xin, they'd tear down his house. Old Xin was quick to agree. He'd borrow the money that afternoon. Xiaoli asked his wife about Song Caixia. Before Song agreed to marry her brother, Old Xin's wife told her, she'd spent three days at their house, where they'd had long talks at night. Song said she was from Youtang hamlet in Qinhan County's Weijin Township. That was what was on Song's ID, which Xiaoli had seen. Old Xin's wife was from Mingchao hamlet in Songdai Township. No more than fifty *li* separated them, close enough to say they were from the same hometown. With this information, the four of them analyzed the situation. Where would Song go with the money she scammed from the Niu family, which was, minus the 3,000 yuan for Old Xin's wife, 97,000 yuan? They all agreed, as Old Xin's wife had said on the floodplain, that she must have gone back to her hometown. She could have gone somewhere else, but they knew where her family lived, so they could find her through them. And if her family did not know where she was, they owned a house that must be worth 100,000 yuan. So, Xiaoli was going to Qinhan. She and Old Xin's wife agreed to take a local bus to the county seat, then another bus into the city, where they would board a train to the capital, switch to a local bus to Qinhan's County seat, and from there take a village bus to Weijin Township, and finally to Youtang Village.

Xiaoli arrived at the bus depot at 7:30 in the morning. At eight o'clock Old Xin's wife still had not shown up, and Xiaoli started to worry that the woman was not to be trusted. The first bus to the county seat left at 8:15 a.m., and there was no appearance by Old Xin's wife. By nine o'clock there was still no sign of the woman. Xiaoli took out her phone to call Feng Jinhua and have him go to Xin Clan Village to pull down Old Xin's house, then finish up by throwing both him and his wife into the river. She'd just dialed the number when she spotted Old Xin's wife, a large woven bag over her shoulder and a big handbag in one hand, wobbling her way toward her. She breathed a sigh of relief. "Everything's fine," she said into her phone.

Old Xin's wife walked up to Xiaoli, breathing hard: "Am I in time?"

"In time? Are you serious?" Xiaoli said unhappily. "The first bus left a long time ago, and the next one won't leave for another hour."

At that moment, Xiaoli spotted a little boy behind the woman. His face was sweaty, and his nose was running; he was holding a little pinwheel in one hand and hanging on to the woman's clothes with the other. He was staring at Xiaoli, who was momentarily speechless.

"Who's this?"

"My son. Since we're going to my hometown, he can come along and visit his grandparents; he hasn't seen them in three years."

Niu Xiaoli did not know whether to laugh or to cry: "We're searching for someone, not sightseeing. We can't take a kid with us."

"He won't be in the way."

Before Xiaoli could say anything, the woman made a case for the boy: "He's not even four feet tall, so he'll travel free."

Once again, Xiaoli was stumped for words. Even if the boy could travel free, the trip would be a lot harder with a child tagging along. If something happened at a critical moment during their search, they couldn't be saddled with worrying about him. She had said no when Banjiu wanted to come along to ride the train, and now here was Old Xin's wife bringing her son along. Free tickets or no, he would have to eat, and who would be responsible for that? It would have to come out of the 3,000 yuan Song Caixia had given Old Xin's wife for being a broker, though now it belonged to Xiaoli. Apparently able to tell what was on Xiaoli's mind, Old Xin's wife opened her handbag, which was filled with fried flatbreads.

"I worked it out. With six buses and trains, we're talking five days to Qinhan. These flatbreads will be enough for the three of us."

She handed one to Xiaoli. "Try one."

For the third time, Xiaoli could only shake her head. She had no choice but to break off a piece and put it in her mouth. It was still warm, and slightly sweet, with the added flavors of green onions and sesame salt. It tasted good.

"Well?" Old Xin's wife said.

"Not bad. Did you make them?"

Old Xin's wife nodded. "I was up most of the night making them."

She patted the large woven bag. "And I've got a dozen large leeks in here."

This conversation proved to Xiaoli that Old Xin's wife was a woman to reckon with. Though undersized, she was not afraid of hard work and knew how to plan ahead. As the adults talked, the boy sniffled and started running around the station, spinning his pinwheel, and shouting *du-du*, mimicking the sound of a motorcycle.

"How come I didn't see him when I was at your house?" Xiaoli asked.

"I can't keep him in the house. He's always climbing village trees to dig through birds' nests."

A thought occurred to Xiaoli: "What's your name?"

"Everybody just calls me Old Xin's wife."

"Don't you have an actual name?"

"Zhu Juhua," she said with a shy smile:

"How about him?" Xiaoli pointed to the child.

"His dad named him Xuewen, but everyone calls him 'Little Monkey.'"

Xiaoli chuckled; the boy did look like a little monkey as he scampered around the bus depot. Then another thought popped into her head: "Did you bring the money?"

At the mention of travel money, Zhu Juhua set down her bundles, undid the sash around her waist, and reached inside her pants, startling Xiaoli.

"What are you doing?"

"Three thousand yuan is a lot of money, so I sewed a pocket inside my pants to keep it safe."

That made Xiaoli laugh. The woman really did know how to plan ahead. She reached out to stop her. "Just leave it there. You can take out what we need along the way."

Juhua kept her hand in her pants. "You trust me?"

"I'm not worried that you'll take off without me. Your husband is still back there, and if you run, he'll wind up in the river and your house will be gone."

Juhua chortled. "You're a clever young woman," she said as she gave a thumbs-up.

"What does that mean?"

"Whoever's holding the money is responsible for it."

Xiaoli laughed. She was even more convinced that Zhu Juhua had a good head on her shoulders.

Once they were on the bus, Xiaoli watched the garment factory and bathhouse recede into the distance, which sparked anew her loathing for Song Caixia. She'd never even been to their provincial capital, and now she was going to travel across several provinces, a trip of more than four thousand li. The distance was not as big a problem as her unfamiliarity with the locale. There was no telling what she might run into, and that was a dreadful thought. She had begun to feel sorry for herself. Her father had died before his time, her mother had run off with another man, her brother was worthless, so she had to take care of whatever came up despite being a girl. As she sat there sighing to herself, Zhu Juhua leaned over and said: "I have to thank you, my girl."

"What for?"

"This trip gives me the chance to be away from Old Xin for a few days."

Taken aback, Xiaoli quit sighing. "Are you unhappy with him?"

Juhua just nodded.

"You looked like you were getting along fine when you were carrying bricks yesterday."

"He gets on my nerves."

"Why is that?"

"He's short, and he's worthless, like Wu Dalang. That's why he couldn't find a local wife."

Xiaoli found that funny but didn't want to embarrass her by laughing: "He seems like a good worker."

"He doesn't trust me."

"How's that?"

"He controls the money. I get only 20 yuan a month for me and Little Monkey. What can I do with that little bit of money? I didn't even have enough to buy paper for my days of the month. What does that make me but a beast of burden?"

Xiaoli sighed emotionally: "Who could believe that a shrimp like him could be such a tyrant?"

"Know why he's like that?"

"No, why?"

Juhua looked down at Little Monkey. Since he had no ticket, she had to hold him in her lap. He had run wild in the bus station but fell asleep on the bus. She leaned over and whispered, "I know you have a boyfriend, so I can share this with you."

"What's that?"

"He can't get it up at night."

"So what?"

"A man who fails at night turns cruel in daylight."

Xiaoli was shocked, partly because Juhua was so blunt in front of a stranger and partly because in such a short time she felt she could say anything to Xiaoli. She pointed to Little Monkey: "Then where did he come from?"

"I brought him into the marriage."

Now Xiaoli understood: "Then why try to save him yesterday when he was in the river?"

Juhua slapped her hands together: "If I hadn't, he'd have thrown me into the river after you people left."

"Everyone's got troubles," Xiaoli said to herself silently, with a sigh. "Who knew."

Juhua assumed she was talking about Old Xin: "It's what they mean when they say you can know someone, but not know what's in his heart."

A thought occurred to Xiaoli: "There's something I've been trying to understand the past couple of days."

"What is it?"

"When Song Caixia pulled that marriage stunt, we only gave her 100,000 yuan, but Old Si from Si Clan Fortress was willing to give her 140,000 yuan. Why didn't she pull the stunt on him instead of us?"

"He did offer that much but wanted to give it to her in installments. So, she said no."

Xiaoli nodded. Song Caixia, the scam artist, had left nothing to chance.

6

The three travelers took the bus from town to the county seat, where they switched to a second bus into the city without taking a break. Ten li out of town they fell into line behind a mass of vehicles where roadwork was underway. Little Monkey, who was in his mother's lap, gazed out the window for a while before complaining that he was hungry. His mother took a flatbread out of her bag and handed it to him. When he finished, his head sagged and he fell asleep. It was nearly nightfall by the time they reached the city, owing to the stop-and-go traffic. As soon as they were in the station, they boarded a local bus to the train station. The lights were on. Xiaoli had Juhua take 400 yuan out of her pocket and stay in the square to watch their bags while she lined up at the ticket window. Everything from high-speed to express to slow trains for the trip to the provincial capital was available. Xiaoli decided on the slow train, the cheapest. At the window, she was told that all the slow train tickets for that day were sold, but there were still tickets available for the next day—standing room only. Seats were available seats for two days hence. Since there was no time to wait, she'd settle for standing room and bought two tickets for the ten o'clock train the next morning. She left the ticket window and returned to Zhu Juhua; she was getting hungry. They had been eager to keep going, and the road repairs had put them on edge, so they'd forgotten to eat lunch. She asked Juhua if she was hungry. She was. So was Little Monkey.

"How can you be hungry? You ate a flatbread on the bus," Xiaoli said.

The two women and Little Monkey walked up to the steps of the square, where they shed their bags and sat down. Juhua took out three flatbreads and a large leek, which she broke into three pieces. They started eating. Xiaoli found that the flatbreads had grown stale in a single day; they'd been soft and aromatic that morning, but now were as hard as cowhide, requiring lots of chewing. She looked around and spotted a row of food stalls on the southern edge of the square, the owners loudly hawking their goods.

"Let's get a bowl of soup," she said, pointing to the stand.

Juhua hesitated. "That'll cost money."

"You know what they say: be thrifty at home, don't scrimp on the road."

"You'd have to spend even more if you didn't take care of yourself and got sick," she continued.

Juhua gave her a thumbs-up: "You are a very sensible young lady.

"I'm happy to have you as a traveling companion," she continued.

Xiaoli led them over to the stalls, where wontons, dumplings, fried noodles, stuffed buns, congee, spicy soup, mutton soup, and more were sold. They strolled up and down in front of the stalls, focusing on the soups and stopping to ask the prices. Xiaoli took the lead and sat down at a stall where the mutton soup sold for three yuan a bowl. She paid for three bowls with the money left over from buying train tickets. When the soup came, she dunked her flatbread into it, turning it soft. She dug in, eating with her leek, till her face was beaded with sweat. So did Juhua and her son. The boy did not finish everything, so his mother picked up his bowl, tipped her head back, and drank the remaining soup down. Now that they'd eaten, they needed to find a place to spend the night. They'd planned on taking a train that day and sleeping aboard, but the delay made it necessary to find beds. An inn would cost money, but the alternative was to sleep on the street. Seeing the pensive look on Xiaoli's face, Juhua said:

"We can sleep in the train station waiting room."

"Will they let you do that?"

"The year I traveled here with the human trafficker, that's what we did."

"There's boiled drinking water in the waiting room," she added, "and it's free."

Xiaoli smiled. Juhua had more travel experience than she did. Little Monkey in tow, they headed to the waiting room with their bags, only to find that the regulations had changed. Only people holding tickets for that day were permitted into the waiting room.

"Tsk-tsk, that's news to me." Zhu noticed the lost look on Xiaoli's face. "That won't stop us," she said. "We can sleep against the waiting room wall to stay out of the wind."

Well, there were already several other travelers with the same idea, she discovered, so they looked for some space. Once they'd sat down, Juhua surprised Xiaoli by taking out a well-used blanket and spreading it over them. Though it was early spring, by huddling together under the blanket, they were not especially cold. Xiaoli fell asleep immediately, after a wearying day. She'd been asleep awhile and was dreaming when she felt something funny on her face. She forced herself to wake up and discovered a hand rubbing her face. Thinking it was some creepy guy, she grabbed the hand and opened her eyes. It was Little Monkey, who had slept on the train all day and was now wide awake; he had stuck his head out from under the blanket and was rubbing Xiaoli's face and carefully scrutinizing it.

"What are you doing, you little creep?" she said with a laugh.

Juhua also woke up, saw what was happening, and had to laugh. As he studied Xiaoli's face, Little Monkey bent down and kissed it.

"Pretty," he said.

Xiaoli was amused: "You're only four years old, you know?"

"Little Monkey isn't the only one who thinks you're pretty," Juhua said. "I do too."

"What makes me pretty?" asked a bashful Xiaoli.

"I can't say. it's just different from other people."

"Different how?"

She slapped her palms together. "Big eyes, a large mouth, a high nose bridge, just like a Westerner."

Back to sleep. No more talking. Xiaoli was still asleep as dawn broke and she had to be poked awake. She opened her eyes. It was a sanitation worker, an overweight woman wearing a surgical mask who was poking people with her broom, one after another. Then she swept the area where each person had slept, raising a cloud of dust, which sped up the wakening process. Our three travelers picked up their things and moved over to the center of the square to avoid the dust cloud. Xiaoli and Juhua took turns going to the public toilet in the north corner and watching their belongings, after which they rinsed their mouths and washed their faces in the water fountain on the eastern corner. Then they made their way back to the row of stalls on the southern edge, where Xiaoli ordered three bowls of millet congee with pickled turnips at one yuan a bowl. Juhua took out flatbreads for breakfast. The hot congee warmed them up from the inside, after which they returned to the steps and sat down to occupy themselves watching people. When the station clock struck eight, the travelers walked over to the gate. Since they were holding standing-only tickets, they lined up two hours early in order to board as soon as arriving passengers disembarked to find a good spot to stand. The gate opened at 9:40 a.m.; after their tickets were checked, they squeezed their way into the station, ran to the overpass, crossed it to the other side, rushed to their gate, and were first in line on the platform. Xiaoli and Juhua were breathless; Little Monkey seemed unaffected by the mad dash. He runs around the village every day, Juhua had said, climbing trees to dig through birds' nests. He gets enough practice to be good at this, so it's nothing to him. Xiaoli laughed. Ten minutes later, the train entered the station. Xiaoli watched it till it stopped; by looking in the windows, she knew they'd wasted their time—the cars were packed, and more people got on than stepped off when the doors opened. They were carried aboard, along with their belongings, to a space between cars, and were immediately immobilized. Where did they all come from? Xiaoli wondered with a sigh. All these people traveling south or heading north, scrambling all over and for what purpose? "It's a good thing we lined up when we did and ran to the platform," Juhua said. "Otherwise, we'd never have gotten aboard." Xiaoli looked down at the platform and saw all the people who hadn't made it onto the train and were being pushed back by attendants so the doors could close. The train began moving. Having so many poor people in the world is a bad idea, Xiaoli thought, forced to buy cheap tickets so they can squeeze onto a train; but she was glad they'd done what they did. Banjiu had wanted to come along for a train ride. Xiaoli was glad that she'd said no; otherwise the girl would be crushed flat.

The train made stop after stop along the way, from morning to night, and the car remained jam-packed. The flatbreads they'd brought saved them from going hungry. At first, just standing there being squeezed bothered them the most, but the need to use the toilet changed that. One would stay with Little Monkey while the other elbowed her way through the crowd to the toilet. Then it was Little Monkey's turn, accompanied by his mother. Everyone needed to use the facilities, so the wait was nearly an hour, and even that was no guarantee. They rode for two days and one night, having to hold it in most of the time, until the train pulled into the terminal station. They climbed down off the train, ran out of the station, and headed straight for the public toilet. On her way out of the facility, Xiaoli looked down at her legs, which had swollen to nearly twice their size, so puffy she made indentations with each touch of her finger. Juhua did not suffer the same problem, while Little Monkey was so unaffected that he was already running around with his pinwheel. It was obvious to her that Juhua and her son were holding up a lot better than she was. It had just rained in the city, where gusts of wind chilled the air. Xiaoli and Juhua layered themselves with warm clothing, after which Juhua did the same for her son. They slept that night huddled together against the train station wall. The next morning, they took a city bus to the bus station. The long-distance bus to Qinhan was no more than half full, so Little Monkey, who had no ticket, could sit in a vacant seat between the two women. They had plenty of room to move, unlike the train that had brought them there. Xiaoli could see that few people were on their way to Qinhan, an out-of-the-way destination. As the bus pulled out of the station, she saw scenery that was a far cry from her flatland home some four thousand li away. Here, one mountain range followed another, with one tunnel after another. Little Monkey had been feeling fine in the city, but now that they were on the road he suddenly spiked a fever. Though it happened on the bus, Xiaoli said to Juhua it was probably a result of being stuck on the train, between two cars, where cold wind had hit them from below, and even though it wasn't cold, they and everyone around them sweated from the close quarters. Little Monkey had slept nearly the whole way, waking up and falling right back to sleep; he was sweating when he was awake, and he was chilled by the wind when he slept. It would have been a miracle if he wasn't feverish. "If he caught cold on the train," his mother countered, "the fever should have hit him last night; it wouldn't have been delayed till now. It had to be last night when we slept outside the train station after the rain. Even with a blanket over him, the cold ground chilled him." Xiaoli had to agree with her logic. The fever seemed confined to Little Monkey's head until noon, when he was suddenly hot all over. They were just then passing through a county town called Daqing, and Xiaoli recommended getting off and taking the boy to a doctor. Juhua not only disagreed but actually slapped her son.

"If I'd known you were going to do this, you little shit, I wouldn't have bought you along."

Wah! Little Monkey bawled. Xiaoli did not know whether to laugh or to cry. "He didn't mean to do it," she said. "He's four years old." She stood up to get off the bus with her belongings. Juhua stayed where she was.

"I'm not taking him to see a doctor. That costs money."

"What if he dies?"

"He's never seen a doctor in his life. We'll see what happens in Qinhan."

Xiaoli had no choice but to sit back down. After four or five hours, their bus arrived in Qinhan, late in the afternoon. Little Monkey opened his eyes. When Xiaoli felt his forehead, the fever seemed to have broken, and he was back to hopping around as soon as they were off the bus. She was amazed. Juhua told her to watch their belongings while she took Little Monkey to the toilet. Xiaoli nodded. Juhua took her son to the public toilet on the western edge of the square. Xiaoli was thirsty, so she dragged her belongings along with Juhua's over to a nearby food stall where she bought a bottle of water and drank it while she waited. After half an hour, mother and son still hadn't returned. Another half hour passed, then an hour, and still no sign of them. Panic gripped Xiaoli. Picking up all their things, she walked to the women's toilet, where she checked every stall. There was no sign of the mother and son. She walked out, knowing this was bad. Juhua had run off with her son, leaving her belongings behind.

7

Xiaoli opened Juhua's handbag, which still contained a few flatbreads; then she opened the woven basket, from which she removed Zhu's headscarf, a few pieces of Little Monkey's clothes, and the blanket that had covered them all. At first, she was puzzled as she surveyed the pile, since they had gotten along so well on the way over, even becoming friends of a sort as they learned things about one another, sharing all sorts of personal information. They had even slept under the same blanket, so how could she take off like that? It was, she came to realize, all part of Juhua's scheme. All that sweet talk on the road was a trap into which Xiaoli had fallen. Then it dawned on her that while Zhu had left her things behind, the travel money she'd hidden in her pants had disappeared with her. On a trip of more than four thousand li, from their home to Qinhan County, by saving on food and lodging, the three of them had spent only about 600 yuan, leaving some 2,400 yuan. Xiaoli had assumed that Zhu's frugal approach, even putting off seeing a doctor for Little Monkey, was evidence of an unselfish attitude for her benefit. No, it had only benefitted Juhua herself.

Xiaoli had traveled all this distance in search of one person, whom she had yet to find, and now she'd lost two other people. Ten days earlier, she had been tricked by Song Caixia, the wife she'd found for her brother, and now she'd been tricked by Zhu Juhua. Song had made a damn fool of her, and now Juhua had done the same thing. Xiaoli could see now that Old Xin had been right to give his wife only 20 yuan a month, far from enough for her to run off to Qinhan. The way he'd treated her had also been right, for cruelty was all that kept her from deceiving him. She'd stayed with him all that time, finally managing to run off, thanks to Niu Xiaoli and the 3,000 yuan. But then the thought occurred to her that the woman could have taken off anywhere along the way; the travel money was with her the whole time, so why had she waited until they arrived in Qinhan? Of course, while she didn't know her way around other places, this was familiar territory, but not to Xiaoli. That was the key to the trickery.

The next question was whether Juhua had run off because of her or because of her husband. Was it a temporary escape or a permanent one? If it had to do with Xiaoli's situation, it would be temporary; if it was about getting free from Old Xin, it would be permanent. Xiaoli would be a temporary cause, but the result of a permanent escape put her in the thorny position of having to tell Old Xin how his wife had run off. The resolution of that conundrum—finding Juhua—would now take priority over locating Song Caixia. Back in Xin Clan Village, Juhua had told her she was from Mingchao hamlet in Qinhan County's Songdai Township.

So, Xiaoli picked up her belongings and hired a passenger motorcycle taxi at the bus station; tossing her things on first, she climbed on behind the driver, sat on her bag, and they took off for Mingchao hamlet. Juhua wasn't as clever as she figured, Xiaoli was thinking, since where else but her parents' home could she hide? A monk can run away, but the temple remains. Even if I can't find you, I can find your parents, and I'll find you through them. Qinhan County was in mountain country, so soon after leaving the county seat, Xiaoli was riding on twisting, bumpy mountain roads. Her anger at Juhua was reignited. When she got to the Zhu home in Mingchao and laid her hands on Juhua, the first thing she'd ask her would be when she first realized what a fool Xiaoli was, the same question she'd ask Song when she found her, just before grabbing her by the hair, slapping her, and asking if she had a heart. If she found her by a river, not at her home, she'd find a club and drive her into the water, just like Feng Jinhua had flung Old Xin into the river in Xin Clan Village and then beaten him with a club. The difference this time would be that she'd keep Juhua from climbing back onto the bank and watch her choke, even drown. If not at the river, if she had a bottle of sulfuric acid, she'd fling it in her face and watch it smoke as she screamed in pain while the flesh on her face dissolved and dripped bloody drops. She was reminded of how Little Monkey had rubbed her face at the train station that night and said she was "pretty." Was he Juhua's accomplice in her scheme to deceive Xiaoli? Any four-year-old who could put on an act like that would be super crafty. He could not possibly have been complicit in the trickery. One person, and one person alone was guilty of the heinous crime—Zhu Juhua.

Xiaoli recalled that she had only brought 500 yuan with her precisely because she had known Zhu would have 3,000 yuan for traveling. A quick check of her inner pocket revealed that it was still there. But the larger sum had left with Juhua. She then recalled how, at the county seat bus station three days before, Juhua had wanted to hand the 3,000 yuan to her, so she had no reason to suspect the woman of trickery and thought it was a safe hiding place. She'd told her to keep it. If she'd taken the money, none of this would have happened. It also occurred to her that bringing Little Monkey along was proof that this was not a temporary escape. Rather, the abandoning of Old Xin was total, with mother and son both free of him. They would not return to Xin Clan Village. Juhua had told her that Old Xin was not the boy's biological father, that she had brought him with her into the marriage. Bringing the boy had been part of the woman's scheme. But why had she planned on a permanent escape? Juhua had revealed her disgust with Old Xin during the trip, partly over his brutish behavior but also because he was impotent, which in turn is what had turned him into a brute. That thought led her to a question about Song Caixia: had she left her brother because he too was impotent? Xiaoshi was a shrimp, just like Old Xin, and had married someone from another province since he'd had no success finding a local woman. Xiaoli had listened carefully for the sound of activity in the bridal chamber the night of the wedding, and she was concerned when there had been none late in the night. Seeing a furtive smile on the Xiaoshi's face at breakfast the next morning had put her mind at ease. Was that, she now wondered, a smile of success, or the look of a fool? And if it had been success, had it been complete? From Old Xin and Xiaoshi, Xiaoli's thoughts moved on to Feng Jinhua.

Back in their early days as a couple, their favorite activity when they got together had been to read *The Water Margin*, but really only the sex scenes with Pan Jinlian. It would not take them long to engage in their own sexual activity, characterized by an hour of moans and groans. Feng's potency was one of the reasons she'd settled on him as a husband. At the time, Feng had said that Wu Dalang's short stature in *The Water Margin* was a sign of his impotence, and that's what gave Ximen Qing an opening. If Xiaoshi, like Old Xin and Wu Dalang, was a failure in bed, could that be why Song Caixia had run off? If he'd performed just fine, the trip from home and all the trouble caused by Song Caixia and Zhu Juhua might have been avoided. But, Xiaoli said to herself, Song was a cheat whose sole intent was to trick Xiaoshi for money, so she'd have run off whether he was a cocksman or a limp dick. She'd done what she did for money. What was the reason Zhu Juhua, whose husband, Old Xin had control of all the family money, run off? Was it to be free of her husband or was there something else? Xiaoli could not come up with no ideas, and her mind became occupied with random thoughts.

Niu Xiaoli

It was nearly nightfall by the time the motorcycle taxi negotiated the thirty li from the Qinhan County seat to Songdai Village and the seventeen or eighteen li from there to Mingchao hamlet. She asked around and was flabbergasted by what she learned. Neither Zhu Juhua nor her family existed in the hamlet; the surname itself was absent among the Zhangs, the Hongs, the Fans, the Bais, and the Gous. Xiaoli now knew she'd been hoodwinked. And maybe not just her. Old Xin had also fallen victim to the deception, and for all the three years they'd been married, not just a day or two. For the moment, he did not know he'd been deceived. As she stood on the street, Xiaoli wondered what to do next. If Zhu Juhua was not in Mingchao hamlet, where could she be? If she truly was from Qinhan, such a big county, where could Xiaoli, who did not know a soul there, go to find her? Living a lie for three years was enough to create doubts about Juhua's hometown in Xiaoli's mind: if she was not from Qinhan, where was she from? Her accent pegged her as from this province, but where was she among the many millions of residents in all those villages? As she wondered what to do next, the driver of the motorcycle taxi asked, "What now?"

She looked up; the sky was now completely dark. Lights were on in all the houses. Since Juhua could not be in the hamlet, there was no point in staying there; better to return to the county seat. She needed time to think.

"Let's go back."

"Can't be done."

"Why not?" That was a jolt. "Do we have to spend the night here?"

"No, but we can't go back."

"What do you mean?"

"Mountain roads are too dangerous at night."

"We can take it slow."

"Fast or slow, it makes no difference."

"Why's that?"

"Traveling on dark roads is more expensive."

Extortion—it didn't take a genius to figure that out. They'd settled on 80 yuan to Mingchao and back.

"How much more do you want?"

"Eighty."

That dazed her. Eighty out and eighty back, altogether a hundred sixty. Normally, that would not have seemed excessive to her, but she had a total of 500 yuan on her, all of which she needed to run down Zhu Juhua and Song Caixia. A hundred and sixty yuan was a big chunk of that.

"That's highway robbery. I can only give you twenty more."

"For twenty I'll just leave you here."

"Okay, leave me here, I'll walk back."

"Pay me what you already owe me." He was fuming.

"We agreed on eighty for a round trip, forty each way."

She took out 40 yuan and flung it at the man, who reacted petulantly; he picked it up, dumped her bag on the ground, and sped off down the hill. Xiaoli picked up her bag, draped it over her shoulder, and walked out of the hamlet onto the mountain road. She rounded a bend after walking a couple of li, and there was the motorcyclist, on his haunches, smoking a cigarette near his motorcycle. She walked by without even looking at him. He hopped on and rode up next to her.

"Let's add sixty, okay?"

"I said twenty, so twenty it is."

"How about forty?"

She ignored him.

He spat on the ground: "You're the most miserly person I ever saw."

Xiaoli paid him no attention and kept walking. Finally, unable to hold out, he rode up to her and, with a clap of his hands, said:

"A good man doesn't fight a woman. Hop on."

"Twenty plus today's forty," he added. "Give me sixty."

"Sixty," he concluded, "is better than going back empty-handed."

These comments suggested to Xiaoli that he was not devious, so she tossed on her bag and sat on them. He raced the engine and took off down the mountain road, riding faster than in daylight, scaring Xiaoli.

They did not arrive in Qinhan until after midnight. Xiaoli got off, handed him 60 yuan, and took her bag to walk off … … but where to? The only familiar spot in town was the bus station, where she'd landed from the provincial capital. So, that's where she headed. The waiting room was closed when she got there, suddenly very hungry; she realized she'd gone without food since morning. But now, after paying the motorcyclist, there was only 400 yuan left, making her funds tighter than ever. A restaurant was out of the question. Reminded of the remaining flatbreads in Zhu Juhua's handbag, she sat down on the steps, took one out and, after getting a leek from the woven bag, began to eat. The flatbread did not feel tough as she worked her teeth hard, likely because she was so hungry. At the same time, she was reminded of how the three of them had eaten the first flatbreads at the train station back home, dunking them in bowls of mutton soup, until their faces were sweaty. Now, after swallowing the last of the dry flatbread, Xiaoli went over to a faucet east of the station and drank as much water as she could handle. Then, picking up her things, she went looking for a place to sleep. A hotel would cost too much, but there was a 24-hour store across the street, which would make the bus station safer, like train stations along the way, so she sat beneath the station overhang, took out Juhua's blanket, and covered herself. A trash picker walked past with a length of heavy wire spearing windblown paper. After she passed by, Xiaoli felt she'd seen the woman before. Her size and mannerisms resembled her mother, who had left home eight years earlier and hadn't been heard from since. Someone had reported spotting her in a Xi'an night market; then how had she wound up here? With a start, Xiaoli threw off the blanket, ran after the woman to get a closer look. It was not her missing mother. The woman gave her a puzzled look before Xiaoli walked back, covered herself once more, and sat there resting, once again berating herself for driving her mother away when she was fourteen. However immoral, she was still her mother. Did it even matter if she was immoral? If her mother hadn't left, Xiaoli would not have had to assume all the responsibilities at home. Nor would she be sleeping on the street in front of the Qinhan bus station, four thousand li from home, eight years later. These thoughts drove her to tears.

"Fuck you, Niu Xiaoli!" she raged.

8

Niu Xiaoli slept through the night and was greeted with a stomachache the next morning. At first, she thought it might be her period, but then a rumble down below, followed by an urgent sensation, signaled the onslaught of diarrhea. Quickly flicking off her blanket and picking up her things, she ran to the public toilet on the west edge of the square. It was the very toilet from which Zhu Juhua and Little Monkey had gotten away from her the previous afternoon. As soon as she was inside, she left her things on the sink, dropped her pants, squatted, and let go. After being worn out for several days, she said to herself, and spending the night on cold ground under the bus station overhang, dead to the world, while chill winds blew, she had gotten a cold, like Little Monkey spiking a fever on the road. Then, in order to economize, she'd eaten a stale flatbread and washed it down with cold water from an outdoor faucet. If she'd had a bowl of hot soup to warm her stomach instead, she'd be in better shape. She regretted saving that little bit of money so far away from home, denying herself proper food, and paying the price physically. She understood perfectly the saying she'd used, "be thrifty at home, don't scrimp on the road," but she was trying to find two people with only

400 yuan in an unfamiliar county, and had to conserve her resources. Feeling better after relieving herself, she walked out of the toilet, stuffed the blanket into the woven basket, and headed to a pharmacy, where she spent four yuan on berberine pills, an herbal product for diarrhea. She took four with a glass of hot water supplied by the pharmacist. Back outside, she next decided to deal with her hunger, and not with stale flatbreads. She went to a stall on the southern edge of the square, where she spent three yuan on a bowl of wontons. Her stomach felt much better when she was finished. Her mind was clearer too. Time to organize her thinking about the search. She realized that she had made the mistake of putting the cart before the horse the day before. Why had she traveled all the way to this province in the first place? To find Song Caixia. For what reason? To get her money back. Before she could find Song, Zhu Juhua had run off the day before, making her so angry she changed her plan to make Zhu the target of her search. Zhu had lied about where her home was, so Xiaoli had made this trip in vain. Now that she was thinking clearly, she decided that finding Song was more important than going after Zhu, who had only swindled her out of 2,400 yuan, while Song had absconded with 100,000 yuan. Dropping her search for Song to hunt down Zhu was like laying aside a watermelon to pick up sesame seeds. Naturally, dealing with Old Xin when she returned home would be a cause for concern, but she could not be bothered about that now—more important to worry about herself, which she decided to do by focusing on her search for Song. Xiaoli had seen Song's ID card, which listed her hometown as Youtang hamlet in Qinhan County's Weijin Township. Zhu Juhua had confirmed that. Xiaoli found out from the wonton peddler that the hamlet was a little over forty li away, five li closer than Zhu Juhua's so-called hometown. Without a moment to waste, Xiaoli hired a motorcycle taxi at 70 yuan for a round trip, laid her things onto the seat, climbed on and sat on them, and they were off to Youtang hamlet.

Again it was a mountain road, but newly paved, which made it a smooth ride. They arrived two hours later at a tiny hamlet of roughly a hundred households. After knocking on doors from one end to the other, she learned that no such person as Song Caixia lived there. There were families named Song, none of whom were in any way related to Song Caixia, and Xiaoli realized that, like Zhu before her, Song had made a fool of her. This time, however, she was prepared to be disappointed. If Zhu could give phony information about her hometown, was there any reason to expect Song to have told the truth? She'd assumed that the ID was fake, and now she knew she'd fallen for yet another deception. And yet, since Song described the place in such detail, she could not have made it up; no one unfamiliar with a place could have. She might make up a story, but not the name of a tiny hamlet, and since she had to be familiar with the place, her true hometown should not be far away; another village in the township seemed likely. Song had set a trap for Xiaoli, but it could not be far from the fox's lair. So, she made up her mind to search other villages, and to that end she rode the motorcycle taxi to Weijin, where the township government offices were located. She went directly to the police station. A young policeman was on desk duty. She told him what Song had done, from start to finish, in hopes that he would help her find the deceiving woman. To her astonishment, he responded by saying:

"You know it was an illegal marriage, don't you?"

"Yes," she faltered.

"Illegal marriages are not protected by the law. Did you know that?"

"Yes."

"From a legal standpoint, the woman lived in your house for five days, meaning you held her against her will for that long. That's a crime, you know that, don't you? If she had reported you, we would have rescued her. By running away, she rescued herself, so what are you doing trying to find her? Just so you could detain her again? You would be breaking the law."

Momentarily stunned, Xiaoli finally managed to say:

"She swindled us out of 100,000 yuan, Sir. Isn't that a crime?"

He nodded: "It is, but can you prove it? You say she took your money. Did she give you a receipt? Show me."

Xiaoli did not have a receipt from Song Caixia. At the time, all she thought was, after they gave Song the money, she became Niu Xiaoshi's wife, and they would share a bed; no thought was given to her running off, so why would she have asked for a receipt? She was almost too weak to stand. "I've traveled thousands of li to get here, Sir."

"Near or far makes no difference to the law, only facts and evidence."

"A hundred thousand yuan is a lot of money for us, Sir."

"How am I supposed to believe you without proof?"

"I'm begging you, Sir."

At that, the young policeman ignored her and began playing with his cell phone. Xiaoli walked out of the station onto a crowded street, not knowing what to do next. Yet in the midst of her torment, she had an idea. She paid the motorcycle taxi driver and walked over to a locust tree across from the police station, where she laid down her belongings, sat down, and stared at the station. Reminded of her sensitive stomach, she did not want a repeat of that morning; nothing of the sort had happened on the road, and she'd had no thought for her stomach. The medicine she'd taken earlier was working, which put her mind at ease. At noontime, the young policeman went off duty; as soon as he was out of sight, Xiaoli walked back inside, where a middle-aged man was on duty. He was eating lunch with a spoon and staring at his cell phone.

"I need your help, Sir."

"What on?"

"I've come from Shenzhen for a friend's wedding. Unlucky me, a thief stole my bag with my cell phone on the highway bus. I know she lives in this township, but I forget which village. Can you look her up for me?"

"Call her cell from a public telephone."

"The phone has all my contacts numbers. I can't remember them all."

"What is she to you?"

"A very good friend. We worked together in Shenzhen. I wouldn't trouble you if it wasn't her wedding."

"What's her name?" He put down his lunchbox.

"Song Caixia."

After a glance at her, he spun his chair around to start a search on the computer. Five minutes later, he told Xiaoli that there were five people with that name in Weijin Township, living in five separate villages. Xiaoli took a pen out of her bag, asked for a sheet of old newspaper, and wrote down the five names in the margins, after which she thanked him and walked out.

Next, she hired another motorcycle taxi. Newspaper in hand, she spent most of the day making the rounds of the five villages. Three of the women named Song Caixia still lived in their villages, and none was the one she was looking for. One was a woman in her eighties; the other two had jobs outside the village, but Xiaoli went to their homes and asked to see their photos. Not the one she wanted. Song must have come from a different township. She'd lied about this just as she'd lied about the hamlet of Youtang. It now seemed to Xiaoli that the web of deception was much broader than she'd thought. But based on Song's familiarity with the region, if it wasn't this township, it ought to be one nearby. Xiaoli learned that there were twelve townships in Qinhan County. She had already searched one of the twelve, with eleven to go, She was determined to spend the next couple of weeks turning Qinhan County inside out searching every township until she ferreted Song Caixia out of her hiding place. She began her search at the nearest one, where, applying the same strategy as in Weijin Township, she went to the police station with the story that she had come to attend a wedding. A policeman unearthed eight women named Song Caixia in his township. None was the one she was looking for. By this time, she was down to her last 20 yuan. She phoned Feng Jinhua and told him to deposit 3,000 yuan into her bank account. As soon as he answered the phone, he asked her if she'd found Song Caixia and told her that Old Xin had been there the day before to say he'd had no news from Zhu Juhua since she and Little Monkey went with Xiaoli. He'd tried calling, but her cell phone was turned off, and he wondered what was going on. Feng then asked her if she had spent all the 3,000 yuan Zhu Juhua had taken with her. Why did she need more? Xiaoli had trouble dealing with all these questions, wanting to keep Feng and Xin in the dark. Telling them what had happened would further complicate things. That was why she hadn't told Feng that she had only 500 yuan left, after Juhua ran off. She was phoning only because she had no choice.

"Looking for someone isn't easy, you know," she complained.

After that she said: "I want you to deposit the money—no more back talk."

She hung up. He did not dare disobey, and 3,000 yuan showed up in her account that night. Just to be safe, Xiaoli withdrew only 500 yuan from an ATM; when it was gone, she'd withdraw another five hundred. Cash in hand, she resumed her search of townships. Anticipating a long road ahead, she was determined not to waste her money and would spend what she had on food, a lesson learned from her bout with diarrhea. If it happened again, that would impact her search and her finances. She ate three meals a day, with hot soup. By sleeping outside the bus station every night, she got to know the owners of the stands, one of whom asked her what she was doing each day from morning to night and then bedding down in the station. She told him about the trouble she was having searching for someone. He and a number of passersby were sympathetic, voicing their contempt for Song and Zhu, who had brought shame to the region. Their sympathy did not result in any help, however; nor did it lead to charitable contributions of money. Day after day she searched, and day by day her supply of funds dwindled. In addition to food, she needed to hire motorcycle taxis at 70 or 80 yuan, even as much as 100 yuan for longer trips. In three days the 500 she'd withdrawn was gone, so she returned to the bank for more. To save money, she got up at the crack of dawn each day and went out at once, so she wouldn't have to return in the dark, when the taxi drivers would charge extra. Some of the villages were near, others far, but on average she was able to search half a dozen a day. Another three days passed. The sun was still high in the sky when she'd finished searching six villages that day. She checked her phone; it was only 3:30. Wanting to squeeze in as much work as possible, she had her taxi driver take her to a village called Yidaoliang, where there were two women named Song Caixia. She met one and saw a photo of the other—neither was the one she sought. Meanwhile, night had fallen, and Xiaoli was concerned that the driver would want more. But he told her to jump on with no mention of money. The left side of his face was covered with a birthmark the size of her palm. She had read the novel *The Water Margin*, and was reminded of the character Yang Zhi, known as the Blue-faced Beast. As she sat there, she was thinking that this Yang Zhi was ugly, but he seemed to have a good heart, a true "man of the marshes." As they passed through some foothills, the driver abruptly turned and headed down a path into a field.

"Where are you going?" Xiaoli shouted, suddenly frightened.

In a matter of minutes, the crops had swallowed them up. Knowing this was bad, she jumped off the motorcycle. Yang Zhi pulled up and stopped.

"What are you doing?" she demanded

He eyed Xiaoli: "Now that we've spent a day together, there's something I want to talk to you about."

"What?"

"I, uh, like you."

"Don't be ridiculous."

"I won't charge you for today's ride. Let's do it one time."

"No way. My husband's waiting for me in the county seat."

Yang Zhi drew up closer: "There isn't a soul anywhere in the twenty square li of this field. Especially not your husband."

He rushed her, pushed her down on the ground, and pulled down his pants. He was about to take hers off when she began to struggle. "This is against the law. Don't you know that?"

"In this deserted place, only heaven, earth, you, and I will know. Fuck the law!"

She kept struggling: "Then it'll have to wait."

"Why's that?"

"I'm having my period."

"Let me make sure of that." He stuck his hand inside her pants.

"I've got a record of this."

"Of what?"

"I was afraid something like this could happen, so this morning I took a photo of you and your motorcycle taxi and sent it to my husband's phone. If anything happens, he'll report you to the police."

She opened her phone and showed him the image on the screen. Yang Zhi was sitting on his motorcycle smoking a cigarette. His face and license plate were recognizable. Over the week she'd been searching, in order to barter with taxi drivers, she had hired more than one, taking photos of all of them and their motorcycles when they weren't looking; of course, she hadn't sent any of them to Feng, for that would have really complicated matters. Rather, she'd sent them to another number, her own number, one she no longer used, as a precaution. As she'd hoped, seeing his face and motorcycle on her phone took the fight out of him. He climbed off her, put his pants back on, and spat on the ground: "Shit!"

"You bitch!"

He took Xiaoli's things off the seat and threw them to the ground. Then he jumped on and rode off, not even stopping to get paid for the day's ride. With a sigh of relief, Xiaoli got up off the ground, dusted herself off, picked up her bag, and began walking toward Qinhan County, a distance of fifty li. She was still walking when a rooster crowed in a village she was passing. When she saw the lights of the town, she sat down and cried.

Two weeks passed. Niu Xiaoli had visited the police stations in all twelve of Qinhan's townships, attending twelve of Song Caixia's weddings. She'd laid her eyes on about a hundred women named Song Caixia, young and old, even one who was actually a man. She kept at it, day in and day out, until the sight of another Song Caixia made her nauseous; and yet not one of them was the person she was looking for. Could that have been a result of a careless search? Could it be that the records at the police stations were in error, leaving the targeted Song Caixia off the list? Maybe she was from a different county. But if so, which one? Given Song's familiarity with place names in Qinhan, Xiaoli reasoned, she couldn't have come from too far away. Xiaoli bought a map of the area, and found that four counties surrounded Qinhan: Fanghua, Liujie, Fulin, and Songyin. Which one? She vacillated between continuing to look in Qinhan County to determine if her Song Caixia might have fallen through the cracks in her search or move on to the new battlefields of adjacent counties. If the latter, where to start?

Two weeks of searching had produced hardships and dangers, and she dreaded the prospect of going through that again. Clearly, she could call it quits, give up the search, and go home. She had already spent more than two-thirds of the 3,000 yuan Feng had deposited for her ten days before. There was only a little more than 300 yuan left. If she decided to get back on the road, she would need to have him deposit even more and would have to put up with more questions. But if she went home, she would never retrieve the money Song Caixia had tricked her out of. Wasted too were the 3,100 yuan in travel expenses; with interest on the loan, the new total was 122,300 yuan. A further worry was the disappearance of Zhu Juhua and her son two weeks earlier. What could she say to Old Xin? Having spent several days focused on the search for Song, Xiaoli had put Juhua and Little Monkey out of her mind. Now she put it back in, and it really bothered her, since it reminded her that she had to search the province not for one person, but for three. She grew increasingly cross as she sat on the steps of the Qinhua bus station square, not knowing what to do next. She went into the public toilet, where the image looking back at her in a mirror showed the effects of two frantic weeks on the road. Her cheeks had acquired the red tinge typical of people from the high plateau. She rubbed her face and heaved a sigh. She walked back out and returned to the steps, where a woman walked up and sat down beside her.

"Are you from one of the inland provinces?" she said to strike up a conversation.

Niu Xiaoli turned to look at the woman, who appeared to be in her thirties. She wore her hair short and was smartly dressed. Xiaoli had no idea where the woman had come from or what she wanted, but she nodded.

"You're looking for Song Caixia, aren't you?"

That question took Xiaoli's breath away. "How did you know that?"

The woman smiled. "You've spent so much time at the bus station that everyone who works there knows."

Xiaoli sighed: "Two weeks already, and no luck. I don't know what to do next."

"I know where she is."

Stunned by this news, Xiaoli grabbed the woman: "How do you know that? Where is she?"

"She went to another province to get married again."

Xiaoli slapped her own forehead. Of course, no wonder she couldn't find her in Qinhan; she must be off cheating someone else. But then doubts arose: "Even if she went to another province, she was born in Qinhan County, where I've spent two weeks looking for her, without even finding her family."

"She isn't from Qinhan."

"Then where is she from?"

"One of the neighboring counties."

That cleared things up. When she set out on her plan of deception, Song had lied about her home county, not just her home village, which showed how bold she was. Xiaoli was no longer interested in other Qinhan County villages. Since Song had gone to another province to marry again, that's where Xiaoli had to go. She had set her sights on Song's hometown simply as the place to find or find news of her.

"Do you know which county and village she went to this time?"

"I do."

Xiaoli took the woman's arm: "Tell me, please, so I can look for her there.

"If you help me with this, I'll be eternally grateful," she added.

She was shocked by what the woman said next with a smile: "Not so fast."

Xiaoli froze. "What do you mean?"

"We live in an age when information is not free."

"How much do you want? If it's a hundred yuan or two, I'll give it to you right now."

"The wonton seller said Song Caixia tricked you out of 100,000 yuan. Do you think I'm stupid enough to settle for a hundred or two?"

"How much do want?"

"People who sell onions and garlic make a 20 percent profit. Twenty percent of 100,000 is 20,000."

Xiaoli froze. "That's taking advantage of someone whose down on her luck."

The woman got up and started to walk away. "Forget it, then. We can still part on good terms."

Xiaoli reached out and grabbed her. "Let's talk about this."

She added, "Twenty thousand is a lot of money. I don't have that much on me. Won't you take less?"

"I can go down 5,000. Make it a round 15,000 yuan. That's as low as I'll go."

"Fifteen thousand is still a lot of money. I only have 300 yuan on me."

"Have somebody deposit to your card. Easy as that."

Xiaoli began to suspect that this woman also wanted to trick her: "How do you know where Song Caixia's home is? And how do you know she went to get married again?"

"A cousin of mine married a man in a neighboring county from the same village as Song. Yesterday, she came back to Qinhan on a family visit."

That made sense to Xiaoli, and she thought that over. "How's this—you don't have to tell me where she went to get married, just tell me the name of her county and village. By limiting the information, you can lower the price."

The woman laughed. "Don't try to pull that on me. Telling you where her family lives is the same as telling you where she is."

Xiaoli dug her heels in. "If you won't tell me, I'll go ahead and search all the villages in surrounding counties. That's what I was going to do anyway."

"Go ahead. Song Caixia's family doesn't live in one of those counties. I'll tell you that for free. But if you're going to search every village in all those counties, how much do you think you'll spend on food and transportation? Think about it. That'll add up to more than 15,000 yuan."

Xiaoli figured it out for herself. Qinhan was just one county. She had already spent 3,100 yuan there in a couple of weeks. At that pace, it would take her two months to search the other four. Taken together, her expenses would easily exceed 15,000 yuan. The woman had obviously thought this out carefully. And there was more than money involved here. A number of unexpected things had occurred during her two weeks in Qinhan; how many more such things might occur over the next two months? It was a dreadful thought. Working together with this woman would save time and money, for she could go directly to where Song was living, without having to spend another two months looking for her native home. Then the obvious occurred to her:

"Let's say I give you what you ask, and you give me Song Caixia's address. Then I travel to that province, but there's no Song Caixia. I'd have thrown all that money away, isn't that true?"

"I can be flexible if you'll trust me. I'll go with you. When you find Song Caixia and get your money back, you can give me my commission. How's that?"

So the money would not change hands until she'd found whom she was looking for. No hawks in the air till a rabbit is spotted. Xiaoli pondered the offer for a moment. It seemed fair. Not only that, if she quickly located Song and retrieved the money, there would be no need to go through the hassle of having Feng Jinhua deposit more. He'd interrogated her over 3,000 yuan; if now she wanted 15,000 yuan to locate Song's hometown, he'd question her to death. She made up her mind.

"When do we leave?"

The woman laughed: "I like people who don't dillydally. I'll go home and pack. We'll head out this afternoon."

9

That afternoon, Niu Xiaoli and the thirty-ish woman set out from Qinhan's county seat on a highway bus, arriving in the provincial capital just before nightfall. They then took a local bus to the train station, where they were told at the ticket window that there was a train leaving for their destination in half an hour. As they congratulated themselves on their timing, they entered the station just as their train was pulling up to the platform. They boarded and found two vacant seats—more good luck. When the train horn sounded, Xiaoli could not help but think back to the bus and train rides two weeks earlier. She, Zhu Juhua, and Little Monkey had been traveling from home to Qinhan County in much the same fashion. There was hardly any difference in the experience, in the passing scenery, and in the sounds; only her traveling companion differed, with the woman replacing Juhua and her son. To Xiaoli, it seemed like only yesterday, not two weeks ago; at the same time, so much had happened over two weeks that it felt like a lifetime ago. She recalled that she was looking not only for Song Caixia but also for Zhu Juhua and Little Monkey as well. By traveling to another province with this woman, she was leaving Juhua and her son behind. For Xiaoli, finding Song Caixia was the more urgent search. Admittedly, abandoning the search for Juhua meant she would be letting Old Xin down, but she could not be in two places at the same time, so the search for his wife would have to wait. Before getting on the road, she discarded Juhua's bags and blanket at the Qinhan station. A single leek remained in the woven bag, dried out after two weeks. The sight of it made her emotional, but she tossed it into a trash receptacle. She and the woman talked as they rode along; she said her name was Su Shuang, that she was a native of Qinhan, and that she was in the clothing business, traveling around the country to any place where there was money to be made. On this trip out of the county, she intended to take care of some business in addition to helping Niu Xiaoli in her search. The trip would not have been worthwhile solely on the basis of the 15,000 yuan Xiaoli would pay her; the combined business made it profitable. As Su Shuang talked on, Xiaoli got the impression that the woman was frank and outspoken, someone who said what she meant and meant what she said; by not holding back, she put Xiaoli at ease, and by taking her along, Su Shuang proved she was on the up-and-up; Xiaoli would not have trusted her otherwise. And, since Su had business other than helping Xiaoli, she need not feel overly indebted. By rights, she should have paid Su Shuang's traveling expenses since she was helping her locate someone; before setting out, however, Su suggested that they pay their own way. At first, Xiaoli felt she should pay, but she now had a clear conscience.

The next afternoon, they arrived in the provincial capital after a fifteen-hour ride. Xiaoli thought they would take a bus to Song Caixia's new home right away, but Su Shuang said she had some business in the city to take care of first. She had been clear about the other business on their way over, that helping Xiaoli in her search wasn't the only reason she was making the trip, and, to top it off, she was paying her own way. Xiaoli did not feel right in forcing the issue about heading out at once. She had something to take care of, but so did Su; so even though Xiaoli felt that hers was more urgent, the clarity on the train made it impossible for her to force the issue. So, first she would tag along as Su took care of her business. Xiaoli took note of the woman's cleverness; by making things clear at the outset, she was not only being frank and direct, she was also giving Xiaoli a heads-up. Su hailed a taxi. Xiaoli assumed they would be going to a garment factory or department store since that was her business, and so she was surprised when they drove for forty minutes and stopped at a hotel where Su Shuang walked up to the reservation desk and took a room. She asked Xiaoli for her ID card.

"I can't afford to stay in a hotel like this, Su Shuang."

Su smiled. "I've taken a double room, and you don't need to pay. But you do need to register."

Xiaoli handed her ID card to Su Shuang, who gave it back after they checked in. They carried their belongings up to the room, where Su went into the bathroom to take a shower. When she was finished, she came out with a towel wrapped around her head and said to Xiaoli:

"Your turn. You'll feel a lot better after a hot shower."

Xiaoli went in, stripped, and showered. She needed it. She hadn't had a good wash since leaving home two weeks before. All that time she'd spent sleeping outside train and bus stations, washing up with cold water at public faucets. No bathhouses for her. She turned on the shower, sighed, and luxuriated in the spray of hot water, which opened up her pores. The water was still piping hot, and she was sweating within two minutes. She began to scrub, sending clumps of dirt flying. After a glance to make sure the bathroom door was securely shut and locked, she really began to scrub and rinse, washing her hair with shampoo and her skin with shower gel. When she was done, she felt pounds lighter; she was like a new person. She cleaned up her mess, wrapped a towel around her, and left the bathroom. She looked at a mirror on the wall opposite the bed and was rewarded with the sight of a healthy glow. The high plateau sun had tinted her cheeks red, as if rouged. When she saw that Su Shuang was looking at her, she responded with a shy smile. She took a change of clothes out of her bag and went into the bathroom to get dressed. By the time they had finished everything, night was falling. Su Shuang said that friends had invited her to dinner and that Xiaoli was welcome to come along. Xiaoli hadn't given any thought to dinner. She asked when Su Shuang was going to take care of her business, so they could go looking for Song Caixia. Su said they were going to talk business over dinner and that they'd get on the road the next morning.

Xiaoli felt better, but she said: "I don't think I'll join you for dinner. I'll wait for you here at the hotel."

"Why?"

"I shouldn't be sitting there while you're discussing business."

"We'll only be talking about reselling clothing, not making drug deals. We have nothing to hide."

Xiaoli was hesitant. "I'm a country girl who doesn't know how to talk to people. I'd just embarrass you."

Su Shuang chuckled. "We buy and sell clothes, not royalty."

How could Xiaoli continue to say no after that? So she went out with Su Shuang, who had called another taxi. A half hour later they pulled up in front of a restaurant on the bank of a river, where they were greeted by two young women, Su's "friends." In their early twenties, one had short hair, the other wore hers in a ponytail, and both were dressed plainly. Su introduced them: the one with short hair was Wang Jinghong, and the one with a ponytail was Li Boqin. They immediately took her hands in theirs and began talking. They appeared to be quite friendly, which put Xiaoli at ease. They walked into the restaurant and were seated in a private room with a copper hot pot in the center. A fire was already heating the water, awaiting the addition of sliced lamb and beef, fish balls, tripe, tofu, noodles, cabbage, and more arrayed around it. Wang Jinghong asked Xiaoli where she was from, how old she was, and what she did back home. She told them she worked in a garment factory in town. Wang and Li blurted out excitedly:

"So do we."

While they were enjoying their hot-pot meal, Wang asked Xiaoli what she'd come to town to do. She told them about her search for Song Caixia, how she'd lost Zhu Juhua and Little Monkey, how she'd looked all over Qinhan County, how she'd met Su Shuang, and how they'd traveled together, leaving out nothing. Both girls stopped eating and sighed emotionally. Then they turned their attention back to the hot pot, Wang and Li taking turns to fill Su Shuang in on what had been happening in the city. Xiaoli listened as she ate, soon starting to sweat from the spicy food. Wang Jinghong chose that moment to examine Xiaoli closely:

"Your ruddy cheeks make you quite lovely," she said.

Xiaoli pointed to her sunburned cheek and said bashfully: "Too much sun."

She added, "I'm not pretty, not like you."

"The suntan isn't a problem," Li Boqing said. "Stay out of the wind, and the red will fade."

"You have a different kind of beauty," said Wang.

"Different how?"

Wang and Li Boqin said together, "You look like a Westerner."

Su Shuang laughed: "I didn't think she looked Chinese when I first saw her."

That comment reminded Xiaoli how Little Monkey had rubbed her face two weeks before as she slept during their trip to the first province. Zhu Juhua had said something similar. A bald man with a long face stepped into the room just then, and Su Shuang made the introductions. This is General Manager Fu of the garment factory. He smiled at Xiaoli, took off his coat, and sat down to join them. Wang and Li teased Fu about his looks. He tried to defend himself, but, burdened with a slight stammer, he failed to get the words out before the next wave of lighthearted abuse came. Unable to ward off the barbs, he could only force a smile and keep quiet. The uncomfortable look on his face even made Xiaoli smile. Back home, no worker in the garment factory would ever dare to joke around with the boss like that. GM Fu took it all in good cheer. Su Shuang let him eat awhile before suggesting that they talk business. He laid down his chopsticks and followed her out of the room. She was back in ten minutes with a paper bag. He did not return.

"Where's GM Fu?" Wang asked.

"Thanks to all your ridicule," Su said, "he left in anger."

Wang and Li greeted that with more laughter. An attendant entered with a plate of pulled noodles, which he dumped into the hot pot. The four women started in on them. Li Boqin received a phone call during the meal. When she hung up, she said she had to leave early to take care of something. Wang said she'd go with her. Su Shuang asked Xiaoli if she was finished; she said she was, so all four stood up and said their goodbyes. On the way back to the hotel, Xiaoli asked Su if her discussion had gone well; she said it had. Xiaoli was relieved to hear that. Back in their room, they washed up and went to bed. Xiaoli asked what time they'd go to find Song Caixia the next morning.

"There's actually no need to go looking for her," Su said.

That Xiaoli's breath away. "How can you say that? I won't get my money if we don't.

"And you won't get your 15,000-yuan commission," she added.

"Even if we find her, there's no guarantee you'll get your money back.

"Nor any guarantee I'll get my commission," she continued.

"Why's that?"

"Tell me, is this Song Caixia rich or poor?"

"What difference does that make? She cheated me."

"That's not what I meant. What I'm saying is, anyone who will sell herself has to be poor. No millionaire's daughter would ever do that. And since she must be poor, her family is a bottomless pit. They'll spend everything they get their hands on. It's like throwing a stone into the ocean—it's gone the second you hear the splash."

Xiaoli replied in a choking voice, "What you're saying is, I wasted my two weeks in Qinhan looking for her. The same as coming here with you."

"That's precisely why I say there's no need to look for her."

"That's not what you said back in Qinhan."

"That only came to me while we were on the road."

"What am I supposed to do now, go home empty-handed?"

"I've thought about that too, and I've come up with a solution."

"What is it?"

"You can earn money the way Jinghong and Boqin do."

"Work in a garment factory? You can't make anything doing that. That's what I do back home, and they only pay me 1,800 yuan a month. I'd never be able to earn back the 100,000 yuan she cheated me out of."

"They don't work in a garment factory. That's just what they tell people."

She reached down and picked a paper sack up off the floor beside the bed. It was the sack she'd brought into the room after going out with Fu. She reached in, took out a stack of money, and laid it on the bedside table.

"There's 100,000 yuan here, ten nights' earnings," she said.

Xiaoli was stunned. It only took her a moment to figure things out. She jumped out of bed: "Are you telling me to be a prostitute?"

Su Shuang sneered. "Can a prostitute make that much? Around here it's 400 yuan a night."

Now Xiaoli was really confused. "Then what are you saying I should do?"

"What they do, be a respectable woman."

"What does a respectable woman do all day?"

"Nothing during the day, then she sleeps with a man at night."

"In other words, a prostitute."

"Men of status don't visit prostitutes; it's risky and they're not clean. What they want is respectable women."

"What are men of status?"

"The rich and the powerful."

Xiaoli assumed that the hundred thousand was what Fu gave her when they were outside the room. "Someone like Fu? What is he but a mid-level boss in a garment factory?"

"He's not a garment factory boss, that's just what he tells people."

"What does he do?" Xiaoli was confounded.

"He's a real-estate developer. He may not look like much, but he's worth billions. He's put up buildings all over town."

"So you want me to sleep with him?"

"Not his cup of tea. The money comes from him, but he pays for other men."

"Like who?"

"Men who are richer and more powerful than him."

"Who are they?"

"He needs land to put up buildings, and who controls that? Officials. And buildings cost money. Who has more of that? Banks."

Now Xiaoli understood: "You had this all planned back in Qinhan, didn't you? You had no intention of searching for Song Caixia."

Su Shuang nodded.

"Why did you trick me when you knew how anxious I was to look for her?" she snapped. "Why weren't you honest with me?"

"I had to bring you here so they could have a look at you. Not everyone is 'respectable woman' material."

Xiaoli didn't know whether to laugh or to cry. "What is it about me?"

"GM Fu also said you have a different kind of beauty, like a Westerner."

"How long have they been doing this?"

"Only five months, and they've made seventy or eighty thousand."

Xiaoli lay back down, slowly, and said nothing more. This was too sharp a turn for her. Respectable woman or not, it's still selling your body. She had come all this way to find Song Caixia, who sold her body, though she did it by sham marriages. Xiaoli could not have imagined that she'd travel all this way only to have someone suggest that she sell hers. She was searching for Song over a deception, only to be tricked into coming here. She sat up. "I'm not having any of this. I'm going back to Qinhan to keep looking for Song Caixia."

Su nodded. "Go ahead, nobody's forcing you to do anything. I'm just giving you something to think about."

She pointed to the money. "This will make the search easier."

"You have to pay me for delaying my search several days."

Su Shuang took 10,000 yuan out of the sack and counted off five bills: "From Qinhan to here took four days. I'll give you a thousand yuan a day, another thousand for travel expenses, how's that?"

Rather than take the money, Xiaoli lay back down, thinking that Su Shuang had become a different person, from the frank, straight-talking woman on the train to someone who could be so profoundly deceptive. They'd paid their own travel expenses, both sitting on hard seats and eating out of lunch boxes, making her appear to be the garment reseller she said she was. She'd come with Xiaoli on the search for Song so she could earn a 15,000-yuan commission, she'd said, lumping the two purposes together, which had convinced Xiaoli that she was a real small-business owner. That she spent all her time in the company of rich and powerful men came as a total surprise. In other words, she herself was rich but had acted poor so as not to reveal her real purpose and arouse Xiaoli's suspicion on the road. Xiaoli wanted to rail at her, for she had been so egregiously manipulated, but she knew Su had no desire to pressure her when she laid 5,000 yuan on the bedside table. If she chose not to become one of her "respectable women," she could take the 5,000 yuan in the morning and return to Qinhan to continue her search. She'd leave no worse off than when she came, and the 5,000 yuan for four days would make it worthwhile. That was as much as she earned in three months at the garment factory back home, while in Qinhan she'd told her fiancé to send her 3,000 yuan and had gotten an earful of questions.

With this 5,000 yuan, she would not have to subject herself to more of Feng's interrogations. She'd spent two weeks on a fruitless search, so four days did not count for much, and her anger subsided. Whether to go ahead and do it or not required a yes or a no, and nothing more. Su Shuang, she concluded, was not one to mince words.

Now that she'd spoken her piece, Su turned off the bedside light and went to sleep. She was soon snoring softly, while Xiaoli tossed and turned, unable to sleep. She could head back to Qinhan in the morning and keep looking for Song Caixia. But how to go about it gnawed at her. Su had said that Song lived in a county near Qinhan, and there was no reason to think she was telling the truth. Trying to locate her would mean searching one village after another. Should she retrace her steps in Qinhan to see if she'd somehow missed her quarry or move onto the surrounding counties? If so, where to start? The past two weeks had taken a heavy toll on her, physically and mentally, and there had been dangers to boot. There was no telling what awaited her if she continued her search, and she could come up just as empty after another two months. Each thought added to her trepidation. Su Shuang was right on target when she said that even if her efforts ended in finding Song, neither she nor her family could be counted on to return her 100,000 yuan. A girl from a wealthy family would not engage in a sham marriage, while a poor family spent whatever money that came its way. If Song's family had no money, they did own a house, one that could be sold; but, as the young policeman in Weijin Township had informed her, without proof that Song had in fact cheated her out of 100,000 yuan she'd have no case in a court of law. Both the trip and the search would have been pointless. Her thoughts then turned to the hot-pot dinner that night. How could Wang Jinghong and Li Boqin pretend to be respectable woman, go to bed with men, and still be so happy with their decision? They were pretty girls, beautiful, in fact, so how had they talked themselves into doing it? It occurred to her that this wasn't the first time she'd had thoughts of doing something like that. Not here, but back home, in front of the bathhouse, where she'd told the underground money lender Tu Xiaorui that she'd let him screw her ten times if she wouldn't have to pay back a 99,200-yuan loan, including interest. He'd refused her offer, telling her that he screwed a girl in the bathhouse for 400 yuan, while he'd have to give her nine thousand nine hundred and twenty each time, and that was way too much. If he'd agreed, she believed she'd have gone through with it. Now she'd been told that she could earn 10,000 yuan each time, even more than doing it with Tu. Not only that, with him it would have been a hometown affair; as the saying goes, don't do it if you don't want people to know. She wouldn't have told anyone, but he might get drunk one day and spill the beans. Everyone in town would know in no time. Here she was, thousands of li from home, and she could go ahead without a soul getting wind of it. Those were the thoughts that kept her awake all night. Su Shuang woke up as dawn was breaking. She saw Xiaoli roll this way and that and checked her wristwatch.

"Aren't you leaving for Qinhan, Xiaoli? There's an 8:20 train, I believe, so you'd better hurry over to the station."

"I'm not going."

"Why not?"

"I'm going to do what you said."

Su Shuang clapped her hands. "I knew you were a smart girl and that you'd come to your senses."

"There's still one thing that bothers me."

"What is it?"

"There are prostitutes all over the place. How come you don't take them on as 'respectable women'?"

"I'll tell you, now that you've agreed. We want more than just respectable women."

"What else?"

"Rich and powerful men aren't really looking for respectable women. They can have as many of those as they want. They're attracted to only one kind of woman."

"What kind is that?"

"Virgins."

Xiaoli paused and waved her hand. "I'm not a virgin."

She'd lost her virginity at the age of sixteen, when she and Feng Jinhua were dating. Now at twenty-two, they'd been having sex for six years.

"I won't lie. I might fool you, but not them."

What she meant, of course, was that the men will expect there to be blood. The news had no effect on Su Shuang, who got her drift.

"You're not a virgin, but I can turn you into one."

Xiaoli's eyes nearly popped out of her head. "How, surgery?"

Su Shuang laughed. "To surgically create a maidenhead requires a month of recovery. We don't have that kind of time?"

"Then how do you do it?"

Su Shuang told her that it's sort of involved, but actually quite simple. You put some eel's blood from the farmers market into a tiny sponge and, before sex, insert it, and that's it. Xiaoli was shocked.

"That's cheating."

"Only if you're caught. If they don't find out, then to them you're a virgin."

Xiaoli had to agree she made sense. "How do you keep them from finding out?"

"Distraction."

"What do you mean?"

"You complain that it hurts."

Xiaoli knew that was what a virgin will say the first time.

Su brought her hands together and pointed down below.

"What's that mean?"

"You tighten up."

Xiaoli could see that this was how a man felt that he was with a virgin. The thought occurred to her that when she was bargaining with Tu Xiaorui in front of the bathhouse; he'd told her he'd have been willing to pay a lot if she'd been a virgin. But because she wasn't, she hadn't tried to say she was. If she'd known about the eel's blood and sponge technique, she might have pulled it off with him, and if she'd succeeded, she wouldn't have had to travel all this distance and wind up here. Then she figured that Tu knew all about her and Feng Jinhua's sex life, and, because he knew she wasn't a virgin, was willing to say what he did. She was unable to be a virgin back home, but she could be one away from home.

"Since you can manufacture virgins, why not let prostitutes do it?"

"Rich and powerful men have been around and seen enough people. They can tell who's a respectable woman and who's not at a glance. You have to be a respectable woman before you can be a virgin."

"How could they tell if I was or wasn't?"

"Your sunburned cheeks would tell them you're fresh from a village."

Again, Xiaoli almost felt like laughing. Her sunburned cheeks resulted from two weeks in the sun searching for Song Caixia. She hated them at first, never dreaming they'd do her some good.

"A virgin who looks like a Westerner, that's a money maker."

On board so far, Xiaoli asked, "Will they wear a condom?"

"Why would they do that? It's all about the sensation."

Somewhat worried, Xiaoli said, "What if I get pregnant?"

Su took a package of pills out of her purse. "Take one of these afterward."

"What if I get a disease?" Xiaoli was still worried.

Su took out a blister pack. "Take one of these afterward."

Xiaoli was appeased. "I'll tell you straight out—I'll do it ten times, no more, enough to earn what Song Caixia took. Then I'll go home."

Ten times, the same number she'd given Tu Xiaorui.

"You can leave whenever you want. You can also stay as long as you like. If you stay and then want to leave, go ahead. You're free to come and go; that's how I deal with people who work for me."

She continued, "There's plenty of competition for this job, and I can't guarantee you'll have more work, even if you want it."

Xiaoli smiled shyly.

10

Xiaoli received her first client the next night. She was understandably nervous. Despite the six years of a sexual relationship with Feng Jinhua, having sex with a complete stranger was different. She did not know what the man would look like—tall, short, fat, or skinny, what sort of temperament, what he liked to do in bed, how big he was—which made preparation impossible and her approach unpredictable. Even more nerve-racking than entertaining a stranger would be her success in pretending she was a virgin. Even though Su Shuang had given her two tricks—complaining of pain and making it tight—she had no actual experience and hoped she wouldn't make a mess of things. In the hotel, Su had instructed her on how to engage the client in conversation. Then she'd had her lie down and take off her pants so she could teach her how to insert the blood sponge. Xiaoli spread her legs to let Su insert it deep inside. After checking to make sure it would stay, she took it out and then reinserted it, altogether three times. "Got it?" she asked.

"Let me try."

Su Shuang let her practice. She mastered the trick after nearly a dozen attempts. Before they left the hotel, Su handed Xiaoli a plastic bag containing several blood sponges:

"Tell him you need to use the bathroom before you start and insert one of these."

Xiaoli put the bag in her purse and nodded.

Su told her not to use makeup or wear low-cut or fashionable clothing. She had her wash and dry the clothes she'd worn on the road and put them back on. A respectable woman should look like one, she said. That simplified things for Xiaoli, and by wearing her own clothes, she could move naturally. Wearing makeup and revealing clothing would even have altered the way she walked.

A car came for her at five that afternoon. Maybe, she thought, it was GM Fu's car, which was either taking her to another fine hotel or to someone's house to meet the client. She was taken to neither a hotel nor a residential district, but driven out of the city. The driver, a young man in dark glasses, drove without saying a word on the way. He looked too intimidating for her to ask where they were going. When they reached the outskirts, they turned onto a winding mountain road, leaving the bustling city farther and farther behind, with only uninhabited mountain scenery and the occasional canyon. Suddenly Xiaoli felt all alone, a woman about to be sold, and she was reminded of Song Caixia, how she must have felt after traveling to Xin Clan Village, where she waited to sell herself. Though Song was her bitter enemy, at that moment she felt a sort of kinship with her.

The car took a side road off the mountain and headed toward a gully. After crossing a mountain ridge, the vista opened up abruptly, with a waterfall up ahead that fed a stream meandering down to the foothills. They drove down a paved road bordering the stream, heading deep into the canyon. A mountain slope facing the sun was covered with blooming peach trees. A classic-style courtyard stood on a broad flatland that spread out from the slope. The driver pulled up to the gate and stopped. He gestured for Xiaoli to get out. A middle-aged woman came up to greet her. Without a word, she gestured for Xiaoli to follow her. A pair of stone lions crouched at the gate entrance. As she walked through the gate, she saw a brass plaque etched with the letters "B-18" on the wall. She did not know what it designated. They passed through a courtyard, then another, much like compounds belonging to landlords in the past. At the fifth courtyard, the woman led Xiaoli into a room with a piano, behind which was a floor-to-ceiling aquarium filled with colorful tropical fish that seemed to be swimming inside a wall. Scrolls with calligraphy hung on walls on both sides. Porcelain vases as tall as Xiaoli stood scattered around the room. The chairs were mahogany, with carved dragons on the backs. After gesturing for Xiaoli to take a seat, the woman left the room. Xiaoli explored the room with her eyes. She'd never seen anything like it. The difference between selling sex in a place like this and in the bathhouse back home was beyond description. After a few minutes, the woman returned with a tray of food. She gestured for Xiaoli to come up to the table after she'd laid out the food, a total of four dishes, two cold and two hot, with a bowl of noodles. The dishes were a cucumber salad, sliced beef, cabbage stir-fried with dried shrimp, and stewed fish. The noodles had shredded pork in chicken broth. She could see that the hot dishes and noodles had been made just before they were brought in, for they were still steaming. The woman gestured that the food was for Xiaoli alone and then walked out. She had been so nervous she'd had only a light breakfast and lunch before the long trip here; she was famished. She hadn't even noticed how hungry she was till the food arrived. She sat down to eat but lost her appetite the moment she picked up her chopsticks, which she laid back down after sampling the noodles. Ten minutes later, the woman came in, cleared the table, and walked out. About that time, Xiaoli's bladder made its presence known; she had no idea where the bathroom was but did not dare stand up and look for one. The woman reappeared, gestured for Xiaoli to get up from the table, and led her over to a door, which she opened. It was a bedroom.

She opened a second door—it was a bathroom, as big as two rooms combined. The woman gestured for Xiaoli to brush her teeth and shower. Xiaoli nodded. The woman walked out. As soon as she was alone, Xiaoli shut the door, set down her bag, sat on the toilet, and peed. She then followed the woman's instructions by taking a toothbrush out of a glass, squeezing on toothpaste, and brushing her teeth. After that, she stripped and took a shower, thinking as she did, that given the grand layout and the elaborate routine, the night ahead was going to be a difficult one. The client might be a coarse bruiser of a man who would pounce on her like a wolf attacking a sheep the moment he saw her. It would be the same as rape and might last all night, a night filled with weird events. She wondered if she'd even be able to leave the room whole the next morning. But he'd spent 10,000 yuan, and he'd have to get his money's worth. Like the character Huang Gai being beaten by Zhou Yu, both sides were willing, and she'd take whatever happened. She hugged herself and shuddered. After showering, she got dressed, walked into the bedroom, and there, in a chair beside the bed, sat a man, nearly frightening her out of her skin. She took a close look. He was in his fifties, fair-skinned, hair combed back, wearing gold-rimmed glasses. She assumed he was another factotum. He surprised her by getting to his feet, walking up, and starting to undress her. He was the client. With no preliminaries, he'd started with her clothes, which made her tremble, and worry that she wasn't acting like a virgin. A case of nerves made her sweat. He stopped what he was doing and smiled.

"You're nervous. So, it's really your first time, isn't it?"

Xiaoli nodded. "It's my first time, Good Uncle."

That was not what Su Shuang had told her to call the client. No matter the age, she was to call him "Elder Brother," and nothing else.

"It's my first time, Elder Brother," she corrected herself.

Then she realized that his sudden appearance hadn't given her time to insert the sponge.

"When I get nervous like this, Elder Brother, I have to use the toilet," she blurted out.

He shook his head and smiled. "Go ahead."

Xiaoli returned to the bathroom and stood near the toilet, where she took a sponge out of her bag, inserted it and made sure it wouldn't come out, and then flushed the toilet. Back in the room, the man was lying on the bed and gestured for Xiaoli to join him, which she did, assuming that it was time for sex. She was not expecting him to take her hand and start a conversation.

"Where are you from?"

Xiaoli said what Su had rehearsed with her: "A mountain region."

Su had said that many of the respectable women came from mountain regions. Xiaoli was actually from a lowland.

"Where?"

Again, Xiaoli said what she'd rehearsed: "I'd rather not say, Elder Brother. I don't want to shame the people there."

He appeared to accept that. He felt her sunburned cheek. "It must be high above sea level, the way your face is burned."

Xiaoli exhaled.

"How old are you?"

Xiaoli took two years off her real age, as instructed: "Twenty."

"Twenty and still a virgin?"

As instructed, Xiaoli said, "I come from a poor family, with lots of sisters, so I have to help my parents in the field. I've had no time for boys."

That answer stopped the client, who took a good look at her. "That shouldn't stop you from falling in love. In *The White-Haired Girl*, Yang and up against the roof of her mouth. She was becoming aroused by his tender approach, and her arousal had the same effect on him. He reached down, parted her legs, and entered her. She shuddered with a touch of nerves.

Now that he was inside, he moved slowly and gently, not roughly at all. After five minutes, he withdrew and examined his organ. Suddenly tense, Xiaoli raised her head to look at it with him. There was blood. He nodded, satisfied. Xiaoli was relieved. He reentered her, but now he thrust in and out like a bull, which stimulated Xiaoli; she was enjoying it, though she could not show it. For him it was a struggle, one that lasted a good hour, nonstop, longer by far than twenty-year-old Feng Jinhua, who was thirty years younger than the client. By this time, it had gotten painful for her, as if he was tearing her apart, just like her first time, when Feng Jinhua had broken her maidenhead. But she had to hold out. In the end, the client began to breathe heavily, as his movements turned rapid. Then, a shout:

"Oh, dear!"

He spurted like a machine gun and then collapsed on top of her. Five minutes later he pulled out, spilling drops of blood and semen from his organ. He kissed her, got up, and went into the bathroom to shower. Xiaoli assumed that he'd want her to spend the night. But he got dressed instead. "I have things to do. You can lie there and rest."

He took a wad of cash out of his pocket and laid it on the bedside table without checking to see how much it was.

"They'll give you your fee before you leave. This is something extra from me."

Then he said, "I'm sorry that's all I have on me."

And then, "I hope your father gets better soon."

Xiaoli was moved. He'd believed the lie about her father. In fact, she'd lied to him from beginning to end, and he'd fallen for all of it. Then she recalled that she'd forgotten to complain about pain and forgotten to tighten up. The client hadn't noticed or cared. She thought she would be subjected to a series of torment and strange demands, which was what she feared most, for the sponge might slip out. She never expected him to stay with the missionary position or for him to engage in such gentle foreplay. Then, when he came, he'd shouted "Oh dear!" and given something extra when it was all over. She got off the bed and helped the client button his shirt.

"What's your name?" he asked her.

Xiaoli hesitated as she wondered if she should tell him or not.

"You don't have to tell me if you don't want to, like with your hometown."

But it wasn't the same as the "mountain region" lie, because she had been moved. And yet, Su Shuang had told her not to give a client her real name. Then the inspiration came. She thought of a name: "It's Song Caixia."

The client wrapped his arms around her naked body: "Thank you, Caixia. Good-bye."

He opened the door and walked out.

After he was gone, Xiaoli went into the bathroom, shut the door, and locked it, and she removed the sponge. It was blood-soaked and dripping. There hadn't been that much blood in it when she inserted it, and she understood that some of that blood was hers. He had injured her inside. There was also some of the client's semen mixed with the blood. She stood in a daze for a long moment, holding the blood-and-semen drenched sponge. Suddenly reminded of something, she laid down the sponge and removed two blister packs from her purse, poked out one from each, picked a bottle of mineral water off the bathroom sink, opened it, and was about to drink when the cell phone screen lit up. Before leaving earlier that evening, Su had told her to put her phone on mute. She saw it was from Jinhua. Checking her messages, she saw that he'd called six times already. She laid down the pills and water to answer the phone.

"Where are you? Why aren't you answering your phone?" he asked.

"I've been busy."

"Song Caixia, have you found her?"

"It's taken me half a month of searching. I found her today."

She could hear the excitement in his voice: "Did you get the money back?"

"We're talking about that right now."

"That's great news. I'll go tell your brother and Banjiu."

She hung up. She did not think she'd lied to him. She had spent half a month searching, and today she'd found her. Even if tonight she was Song Caixia.

Chapter 2

Li Anbang

1

Li Anbang and Zhu Yuchen had been good friends twenty-five years earlier. Back then they were party secretaries in neighboring counties of a certain province. Zhu enjoyed teasing Li at dinner after meetings for county party secretaries held in town. Thanks to his peasant background, Li had tested into college and then made it to his current position one step at a time. Zhu pointed to the food on the table and said, "You're a country boy, so I don't suppose you've enjoyed much fancy food in your life. So, dig in." Zhu puffed on a cigarette and went on to say he was from a cadre family, with a township head for a father, and that he'd eaten in every restaurant in town. Li shot back that he may be a country boy, but his girlfriend in middle school was the daughter of the township head. He hadn't sampled much fancy food, but he did have that at least. Everyone at the table laughed. Zhu's county was famous for its pomelos, of which he would send Li truckloads before the Autumn Festival each year. Li gave half of them to the cadres in the country office and sent the other half to the home for the elderly. Celery was a specialty of Li's county; it was so crunchy it shattered when dropped. When celery was harvested, Li also sent Zhu truckloads of the vegetable. Since the two counties were neighbors, the villagers on the borders had often fought over land. Two people had died on one occasion, an event that made it into the provincial bulletin.

After assuming their official positions, Li and Zhu met with the respective county and village cadres, as well as village representatives, and drew a straight line to separate the two counties, compensating those who lost out after the circuitous borderline was corrected. As for those who started the fight, a few people from each county were arrested and received prison terms. When New Year's came around, Li and Zhu each took his own villagers along to deliver presents of pigs and goats. Two years later, no more disputes occurred. The two sides had never intermarried before, but now men and women had begun marrying across county lines. How close did the two men's friendship become later on? The provincial government planned to build a national highway through Li's county. Something fishy happened before the construction began. In order to win the contract, someone had sent Li two large bags of money. Not knowing what to do with the bribe, he drove at two in the morning to Zhu's county, where the two men sat in Zhu's office and talked until daybreak.

A man with a lecherous bent, Zhu got involved with women wherever he was assigned. During his second year in office, he'd gotten a young girl in his office pregnant. He went to see Li for help. They decided to take the girl to Li's county, where Li himself arranged for a secret abortion at the county hospital. After the procedure, Li set her up for a month-long stay at a remote tree farm to recuperate, after which she returned fresh and fully recovered. After serving four years as party secretaries, the two men were promoted to vice-mayor positions. As they left their county offices, the people praised them as "upright officials," weeping as they circled their cars, unwilling to see the men leave. Even the villagers from the other man's county showed up. Seeing off one's own county official was common, but seeing off someone from another county was virtually unheard of anywhere in the country. The provincial paper publicized the scene, which was also on the lips of residents. Now, serving as vice-mayors, they each had an office on the second floor of the municipal building, which made it easy for them to talk about everything under the sun.

So what happened to ruin the friendship? In May of the third year at their new positions, a major shift in how officials were appointed within the province was announced. The plan was for the mayor to be transferred to another city as the new municipal party secretary, and either Li Anbang or Zhu Yuchen would be selected as executive vice-mayor. While a provincial team was in the city evaluating the cadres, the mayor called Li into his office one night and said that someone had reported to the provincial government that he had accepted two million yuan over the highway construction. He asked Li if that was true. Li's head nearly exploded, not simply because the figure was inflated but also because he had told only one person, and that was Zhu Yuchen, with whom he was vying for the position of executive vice-mayor. Accepting bribe money not only meant he would never become executive vice-mayor but also that he could be sent to prison. He never imagined that his friend could be so calculating; they had been extremely close and had worked together for seven years. Li categorically denied the accusation and also brought up Zhu's illicit relationships with women.

"Whoever made the allegation must supply evidence, or be guilty of slander," Li said gravely. "There won't be any, but I have an abortion record from a hospital."

The mayor was livid, saying they would both suffer over their accusations. Neither man would be promoted and, more importantly, it would affect the mayor's own promotion since he would be seen as having failed in his responsibility as vice-mayors' superior. Other cities in the province would profit from their problem. He had called Li in to tell him not to go off half-cocked and that he would tell Zhu the same thing, to keep from creating complications. He would personally talk with the organizational department at the provincial government. With the mayor's intervention, the potential storm was averted, and none of the promotions were affected. Li remained in the municipal office as the new executive vice-mayor, while Zhu was transferred to another city as its executive vice-mayor, in line with the organizational office's initial plan. But the seeds of discord had been sown. Over the next eighteen years, Li enjoyed smooth sailing in his career: two years after becoming the executive vice-mayor, he was promoted to the position of mayor, in which office he served for three years before becoming the municipal party secretary. The timing was right, and luck was with him; five years later, he was a candidate for vice-governor. But he was told by the organizational office that there was an inside candidate, and that he was included solely for the sake of appearances. He was forbidden from any skullduggery and not permitted to campaign for the office. He obligingly refrained from all activities. On the day before the votes were cast, an unexpected turn of events occurred, as someone traveled to Beijing to accuse the inside candidate, a municipal party secretary in another city, of accepting more than 20 million yuan in bribes. The informer not only named the man but also produced concrete evidence. The central government expressed grave displeasure with the provincial party secretary for recommending such an individual. In the meantime, the People's Congress had to meet on schedule the next day, so the inside candidate was disqualified and his name taken off the ballot, leaving Li as the sole candidate for the position of vice-governor. After serving in that role for five years, he was next promoted to be executive vice-governor.

Zhu Yuchen's ride in officialdom, by contrast, was a bumpy one. He had spent seven long years as an executive vice-mayor before being promoted as mayor, an office in which he served for five years. Finally, after serving as municipal party secretary for another five years, he was transferred to the provincial office as vice-chairman of the provincial People's Congress. He held the same rank as a provincial vice-chairman but had no real power. The title had a nice ring to it, but he had less power than a party secretary. The executive vice-governor, in contrast, had real authority, a voice that carried throughout the province. After eighteen years, one man had risen far higher than the other. Aware that gloating was petty, Li secretly felt vindicated when he saw what had happened to Zhu. Sometimes he said to himself,

"Good is rewarded with good, and evil with evil."

Or,

"The organization office treats people fairly, after all."

Suddenly there were new developments, but nothing that concerned Zhu Yuchen, however, since the People's Congress was the last assignment prior to dying a natural death. The changes affected Li Anbang, and for the better, not the worse. Someone from his hometown served as the secretary for a national leader in Beijing. A man in his early thirties, he held the rank of a section chief and yet, as the saying goes, the turnip may be small, but it grows in a prominent spot; he meant a lot to Li Anbang. They were from the same hometown and were distant relatives. The man worked in Beijing, while his siblings had stayed home in the village. Li personally arranged jobs for the ones who needed them and promotions for those who already had jobs. And he did so without mentioning it to the young secretary, who learned about it from his brothers and sisters. Feeling that Li was someone with a vision and a worthy friend to have, whenever there was a shift in the wind direction, the secretary leaked that information to Li using an ultra-secret "red telephone." These shifts might have been considered minor at the central government level, but they turned into loud drumbeats when the effects were felt at Li's level, playing an important role in his decision-making and follow-up actions.

A couple of weeks earlier, the man had told Li via the secret red telephone that the provincial party secretary in Li's province would be promoted to the central government and that his replacement would be the current governor. The central government office was going through a list of three candidates to replace the governor, and Li was one of them. His heart raced above a hundred beats a minute when he heard the news. He was grateful to the central government for including him as a candidate, but was immediately on edge, knowing that he had only a one-in-three chance of being chosen. He wondered whom they would pick. Then something happened, catching him completely by surprise. The secretary called him on the red phone to tell him that, in a move to conclude the process, an inspection team would be sent to his province in ten days to conduct a careful study of the three candidates. The results of their inspection would have a direct effect on the final decision.

The person leading the inspection was a vice-minister, who, believe it or not, was Zhu Yuchen's college classmate from thirty-five years earlier. Zhu may have been relatively worthless, but some of his classmates occupied important positions in Beijing's ministries and commissions, and that included this classmate. Twenty-five years earlier, Li had often heard Zhu talk about the vice-minister, who had been a ministry party secretary, serving as the secretary to a particular leader, much like the young man from Li's hometown. At the time, Zhu had also said they would ask his classmate to show them around Zhongnanhai if they ever came to Beijing. They had not only been classmates, Zhu had added, but had even been bunkmates in the dormitory. It was truly a case of a storm arising out of a clear sky. After twists and turns throughout the years, Li never imagined that his fate would be in the hands of Zhu's old classmate. Zhu had abruptly regained his importance in Li's mind, coming back to life via a classmate rather than dying a natural death. He and Zhu could have kept out of each other's affairs, if not for the governor's selection.

Now Li's prospects for moving up rested on the results of the inspection team. Of course, the inspection was only the first step, and there was no guarantee he'd get the job even if he passed it, for the central government might have other concerns. But if he failed the inspection, he would not even be considered. And the results of that inspection would be based on what Zhu's old classmate wrote and said. When the man came down to their province, wouldn't it be a given that he'd meet with his old classmate? Rumor had it that he'd played a role in Zhu's promotion from municipal party secretary to vice-chairman of the Provincial People's

Congress the year before. Granted, Zhu's new position was essentially decorative, after which his career would die a natural death, even though it was a high-ranking office. Hardly any of his peers could hope for such a natural career death when they reached retirement age. Some might be appointed chairman or vice-chairman of a provincial People's Congress or political consultative conference, while others might retire from their current position in the city without any further advancement. Now when the classmate met Zhu Yuchen, he would surely ask about Li Anbang, one of the targets of their inspection. What was the likelihood that Zhu would say anything good about Li after eighteen years of enmity? Refraining from saying anything positive would not be as bad as actually deciding to speak unfavorably about him, maybe even to a significant degree. He had falsely accused Li of accepting a bribe of two million yuan when they were vying for the position of executive vice-mayor, hoping to send him to jail. The position of a provincial governor could very well prompt Zhu to allege that Li had taken a bribe of 20 million yuan, enough for a long prison sentence. Since Zhu's career had stalled, and he had become an ornamental fixture, he had nothing to lose. None of this would have worried Li if he were not a candidate for provincial governor, but now that he was, he had turned into the proverbial turtle in a jar—trapped. Even more worrisome was the fact that he could not tell anyone about these worries, for he no longer had any close friends as a result of the lesson he'd learned from Zhu's treachery eighteen years before. After putting down the phone, Li spent a sleepless night but failed to come up with a solution to his problem.

Canceling a meeting at the environmental protection bureau the next morning, he told his driver to take him to the outskirts of the capital city, so he could climb Breast Hills. Lying twenty kilometers southeast of the capital city, the hills looked like a pair of breasts. The highest hill in the area, a mesa peak, was where one had a bird's-eye view of the city, which looked like a sand table or a child's drawing. It dwarfed all the neighboring hills. Since assuming his current position, Li had developed the habit of climbing to the highest point in the area whenever he encountered a setback because it afforded him a new angle from which to think over the issue at hand. But this was different, for there was no need to think anything over and no new angle to be had. If he wanted to keep moving up and assume the office of governor, he had to pass the inspection team's scrutiny. And the key to that was in the hands of Zhu Yuchen's classmate. He had no illusions that Zhu would say anything good about him and would in fact take the opportunity to poison the well. Zhu had not forgotten what had happened eighteen years before, and his own career failures might well have given rise to jealousy over Li's success. With new grievances added to old scores, he would have to be almost saintly not to fabricate something out of nothing or spread gossip. He might even accuse Li of accepting bribes of as much as 50 million yuan. Fabricated lies did not frighten Li. He was more concerned about the possibility of one thing leading to another, like a donkey's tail bringing out a club, and lies giving rise to inconvenient truths, like a sesame seed turning into a watermelon. When that happened, he might not even be able to hold on to his current position, let alone take over as governor. If the issue developed along this line, what awaited him would be nothing but nightmares and an abyss. What he needed to do now was ensure it would get no worse by transforming passive factors into active ones and turning a disaster into a blessing in disguise. The prerequisite for such a quick turnabout was to repair the rift between him and Zhu and alter the nature of their relationship in the shortest time possible. The best result would be if old grudges could be forgotten and the relationship returned to where it was twenty-five years earlier, when they had both been county party secretaries. Li was aware of how unrealistic it was to expect to erase eighteen years of accumulated acrimony in ten days. If that could not be done, repairing the damage to their relationship to the point that it was devoid of bias would be acceptable. In other words, he would not expect praise from Zhu but hoped that Zhu would not fabricate anything to kill his chances. Nor would he expect Zhu to follow the standard of a Communist party member to not use a public office to serve personal interests. All he would like from Zhu was to be as humane as possible. He would be more than grateful if Zhu did not manufacture any false evidence to ensnare him in a phony case.

But how was he going to repair the rift in ten days? How was he going to return moral character to an evil man in ten days? Li racked his brain until it hurt, but he still could not come up with a way to resurrect humanity in Zhu, even after pacing Breast Hill all morning, watching the sun rise from the sand table at his feet to a spot over his head. Then he saw a car come up the hill all the way to the mesa-like top. He saw it was a luxury sedan, a Mercedes Benz. As a provincial cadre, Li was only allotted an Audi, which meant that whoever was in the Mercedes Benz was rich. When it reached the mesa, the car door opened to let out a big dog, followed by a small one. The two dogs ran around happily while a thirtyish, heavily made-up woman got out. One look told him it was either a wealthy woman or a rich man's second wife. Li's driver was about to stop the dogs and the woman from disturbing Li's brainstorming when Li's gaze fell on the dogs and felt a bright light go off in his head and a wide path open before his eyes. It was obviously a mother and her pup, for the small dog had stopped frolicking and ducked under the big one to suckle. Li clapped his hands and said to the driver,

"Let's leave and give them the space."

2

A municipal office received a notice from the provincial government that the executive vice-governor, Li Anbang, would be coming to town at nine o'clock the following morning to inspect the drip-irrigation system at a model field. The office notified the party secretary, Yu Deshui, who arrived at the city limits with the mayor and his entourage at eight o'clock to wait for Li, who showed up with his staff half an hour later in two cars. After shaking hands with the city leaders, Li asked Yu to ride with him.

"You seem very happy, Old Yu. Got yourself another wife?" Li asked with a smile.

"I heard some good news," Yu said.

"What news is that?"

"I heard that Provincial Party Secretary Mao will be promoted."

Li was surprised by how quickly those at the municipal level heard about policy decisions that had yet to be finalized by the central government. News spread at record speed; obviously there were no more secrets in China. But he feigned ignorance.

"Why haven't I heard of that?"

"I even heard that Governor Ju will replace Secretary Mao after he leaves. So, who will be the new governor once Ju becomes provincial party secretary?"

"You'll have to ask people in the central government," Li replied.

"I did and was told it was obvious who it will be."

Obviously, that pleased Li Anbang, for it seemed that everyone considered him the most logical replacement as governor, which in turn meant that he was the people's favorite. But he sighed to himself. Being the people's favorite was useless for an official in China. Whether or not he became governor had nothing to do with how the people viewed him, and everything to do with the central government's opinion. And their opinion was contingent upon the report by the inspection team, whose shadow player was none other than his old nemesis, Zhu Yuchen. Yu Deshui knew only half the story, obviously. Li changed the subject.

"How's it going with the drip-irrigation system?"

The system was a Sino-Israeli cooperative venture Li had worked hard to secure for the county from the Ministry of Agriculture. They had wanted to try it out on a hilly area in the southwest, which had largely hilly topography. It made sense for him to come take a look.

"The peasants received major material benefits," Yu said. "The greatest challenge in planting on hills is irrigation because it's so hard to move water up. Now with the drip system, they more than double their harvest."

"Have there been more night raids on the equipment?"

When the system had been set up the year before, the peasants had no faith in the plastic drip lines laid out like spider webs, feeling they were too much trouble; no one wanted to try them in their fields. In the end, the city and county finance offices allocated money as subsidies, which enticed some of the peasants to install the spider webs in their fields. To the chagrin of the officials, non-participating peasants pilfered the drip lines at night to sell at the recycling station.

"We caught more than a dozen thieves, who were all sentenced to three years or more in prison. Severe punishment is the best solution in troubled times. There have been no more thefts," Yu replied.

They reached the county line, where the party secretary and the county chief stood waiting with their entourage. Li got out and shook hands all around before everyone got into cars and headed to the village where the systems had been installed. When they got there, the cars climbed over a ridge to reach the field, where county and village cadres awaited. Everyone shook hands. Crisscrossing the fields like veins in a human body, the drip lines spread out across undulating hills. Someone from the village had turned on the system for them. The visitors came up to watch water flow silently in the lines and quietly moisten the soil. It was impossible to see from a distance that the field was being irrigated. After getting down on his knees for a closer observation, followed by the others, Li stood up and clapped his hands.

"This is truly a case of 'silently moistening things,' if you get my drift.'"

The men got to their feet and laughed at his erotic use of the poetic line.

"We had to beg the peasants to install the system last year," the party secretary said. Now those who refused are lodging complaints about unfair treatment."

Li Anbang laughed at the comment; others followed.

"I came this time mainly to see if the acidic soil around here has damaged the system. I can see now that there is no problem," Li said.

The Ministry of Agriculture experts had expressed similar concerns. The system had only been used on alkaline or non-acidic soil in the past, while the hilly lands in the area were acidic. Li had just seen with his own eyes that the drip lines stayed dry and intact as water flowed through them, with no sign of corrosion or deterioration.

"Everything's fine. We saw no damage," several people responded.

"Looks like we can use it on a larger scale," Li said.

"Yes, yes, we can." The others concurred.

Yu Deshui, the municipal party secretary, suggested that they go look at the spray irrigation system when they were done here, for it was also Li Anbang who had gotten them the system through the Ministry of Agriculture earlier that year. As a Sino-EU cooperative venture, the Ministry of Agriculture had planned to try it out on steep hills. That particular county had gentle hills to the east and steep hills to the west, which was why Li had the spray-irrigation system installed on the western slope. Placing both experiments in the same county made it easy for inspection and management.

"I hadn't planned on inspecting the spray irrigation on this trip, since soil isn't a concern. But Secretary Yu has assigned work for us and we dare not say no. So, let's follow his orders and go take a look," he said.

Yu and the others laughed. Leaving the cadre from the county and village behind, they climbed into cars and crossed hills heading west. At Xiguan, the county seat, a crowd on the highway blocked their passage.

Assuming it was a public disturbance, Li got out of the car and walked up to see a middle-aged woman sitting in the middle of the road. She was slapping the ground around her and wailing under the gawking eyes of onlookers. It was not a public disturbance after all, so Li pushed his way through the crowd to see what was going on, while the party secretary and county chief looked on anxiously.

"What's wrong, Aunty?"

She was crying too hard to hear him, so Yu came up and nudged her.

"He asked you a question."

Finally, the woman looked up and told them the name of her village. She had come to the county seat early that morning to buy medicine for her husband, but the 2,000 yuan in her cloth bag had been stolen before she reached the hospital. Without the medicine, she was worried that her husband would beat her when she got home, which was why she was crying. Li checked to see how much money he had. It was only 300 yuan, so he turned to Yu.

"Lend me 1,700 yuan. I'll repay you when we get back."

Yu found that he only had 200 yuan. Not the type to spend money freely, neither men carried much with them. The mayor checked his pockets, as did the party secretary and county chief, until they managed to pool 2,000 yuan among the five of them. Li handed the money to the woman, who took it, banged her head on the ground, got up, and ran off. She hadn't once asked who these people were.

"She could be a con artist," the county chief said.

"You have no evidence, so don't call her that," Li said, displeased. "Even if she were, she's poor. Your wife wouldn't do this, would she?" Li added, turning to Yu. "I come from a peasant family, so maybe that's why I can't stand seeing poor people cry."

"I apologize for saying that, Governor Li," the county chief said red-faced.

"We're dealing with class feelings." Yu Deshui tried to smooth things over. "Since he's from a landlord family, he'll treat us to lunch today."

That got a good laugh from everyone.

"I'll notify the public security bureau, and send someone after her," the county chief said.

"You do that," said Yu Deshui.

The county chief took out his cell phone to make the call while the others returned to their cars and continued westward. When they reached the mountain region, they crossed hilly ridges until, more than an hour later, they arrived at a steep hill where village cadres stood waiting. The irrigation system was turned on the moment they spotted the cars; hundreds of sprinkler heads immediately began spraying water, turning as they did to shroud the hill in a watery mist. The crops received moisture from mist that created tiny rainbows under the sun, creating a multicolored spectacle.

"As the saying goes, remember the well digger when you enjoy the water," Yu said, pointing at the rainbows. "It's because of Governor Li that you people will never miss a harvest, come drought or flood. Don't forget that."

They applauded. "Don't listen to Old Yu's nonsense," Li said. "Party Secretary Mao sent me to Beijing to get you this system. He's the one you should thank." They applauded again, after which they stood and watched the rainbows. Then the visitors turned to enjoy the mountain scene, before getting back into their cars for lunch at the county seat. Li and Yu rode together again. Along the way, Li turned to Yu.

"I seem to recall that Director Zhu's old home is located in this county. Is that right?"

"Which Director Zhu?"

"Director Zhu Yuchen of the Provincial People's Congress."

Yu nodded.

"Anyone from his family still living here?"

"His mother died two years ago, but his father's still alive."

"Now that I'm here, I'd like to see him after lunch."

Li had set up the two irrigation systems in this particular county as the most appropriate spots, forgetting that Zhu Yuchen's family was from there. If he had recalled, he might have decided to install them elsewhere. What a surprise that a neutral act at the time could work in his favor now. But Yu frowned when he heard Li's desire to visit Zhu Yuchen's aging father, as if caught in a terrible bind.

"What's the matter?" Li asked.

"I'm not sure it's a good idea," Yu said.

"Why is that?" Li was surprised.

"It could turn ugly if you're not careful."

"What is that supposed to mean?"

"Director Zhu's father isn't just any old man. Taking advantage of his son's official position, he undertakes lawsuits in the countryside and offers his help to fight for the masses. People who go along with him prosper, but those who don't suffer. He's given us endless headaches. He's in his eighties, and I've never seen anyone with so little self-respect at his age."

"Does Director Zhu know?" Li asked in disbelief.

"Director Zhu's father beat the hell out of him as a child, and their relationship hasn't changed since then."

"Are you sure?"

"I heard this from people in the county." Yu lowered his voice. "Once when Director Zhu came home to visit, while people were chatting, he said something not to his father's liking, so his old man slapped him."

Li was staggered. He hadn't expected that someone like Zhu Yuchen, who had the heart of a snake or a scorpion, could be cowed by anyone, especially his own father. It was unheard of that a ranking cadre was constrained by feudal ethics at home. But it was a happy surprise for Li, who realized that he'd made the right decision to visit the county.

"That can't be true. I was told that Director Zhu's father was once a township chief. He couldn't be so lacking in scruples."

"Who told you that?" Yu asked.

"Director Zhu himself. Twenty-five years ago, when we were both county party secretaries, he was always showing me up by saying I was a farm boy who hadn't seen the world, while his father was a township head, which made him the son of an official."

"He was pulling your leg," Yu said with a chuckle. "His father was the village butcher."

Li chuckled too. So, Zhu had lied to him all those years ago.

"Old Zhu is on the road to retirement," Yu added softly. Why are you worried about him?"

Li assumed that Yu might have been aware of the rift between him and Zhu. Since it had gone on for eighteen years, it was not surprising that others knew about it. Yu was probably using Zhu and his father to show Li where he stood. But he only knew half the story; he was aware of the conflict between the two men, but not Li's current attempt to eliminate it, and he knew that Li was more important than Zhu, but he was unaware of Zhu's current importance to Li.

"I want to visit him precisely because he's in a secondary post," Li said. "There'd be no need to see him otherwise. Old Zhu and I have some issues," he added, "but we were once best friends. We're getting old and ought to find a way to get over our past."

Yu was flabbergasted and speechless, but he changed his view after thinking it over for a moment. He gave Li a thumbs-up.

"What an outlook!"

It was hard to tell if he was commenting on Zhu's virtual retirement or was speaking about Li's magnanimity in forgetting past animosities. So, after lunch, the cars took off for Zhu Family Village, where they went straight to Zhu Yuchen's house and met his father. A few words out of the old man's mouth were enough to tell Li that Yu Deshui had told the truth, for he was indeed an arrogant man with little experience to justify his conceit. They had loaded the car with cigarettes, liquor, rice, cooking oil, soft drinks, and a couple of pig's legs.

"Governor Li has come to see you, Gramps," Yu said to the old man soon after they walked in."

Li shook hands with the old man while the county staff carried the gifts inside. With his eye on the gifts, the old man pointed to the party secretary.

"You're no good," he said.

Yu appeared baffled. "What have I done, Gramps?"

"I haven't seen your face for a month, but now that a provincial official is here, so are you. Are you here to see me or to be seen with him?"

The party secretary's face reddened. "I know I could have done better, Gramps. I've been very busy lately."

Then the old man pointed to Li Anbang. "Are you the governor or the vice-governor?"

Now Li knew the old man did not watch TV, for Li often appeared on local news programs. Yu was about to come up and say something to the old man, but Li stopped him.

"I'm the vice-governor, Gramps."

"So does that mean you and my son are the same rank?"

"Director Zhu is part of the provincial People's Congress, which oversees the provincial government office, so Director Zhu is my superior."

Li's answer made sense theoretically and legally because the People's Congress did supervise government offices, though in reality this was just symbolic.

"In which case you came to see me because you need my help," the old man said.

Yu could not stand the man's increasingly insulting tone. "Governor Li came to see you today, Gramps, because he is a good friend of Director Zhu's."

"How come Yuchen never mentioned him?" the old man asked. "No one gets up early if there's nothing to be gained. He just doesn't feel like telling me what he wants."

Deep down, Li had to agree with the old man, so he said:

"I'll come see you in the future if I need your help, Gramps."

"You thought highly enough of me to come see me today," he thumped his chest and said. "If you need help from Yuchen, but you don't feel like asking him, I'll talk to him. He'll do what I say."

The others found him funny yet annoying, but Li said, "I will, Gramps."

He could tell by now that Zhu's father was a simple-minded man, or a frog in a well, someone with a narrow view of the world, which was why he thought so highly of himself. But he was straightforward and no-nonsense precisely because he was that frog, which was what Li had wanted all along, for it quickly bridged the gap of communication between them. It would have been play-acting if the old man had been a calculating pedant and they'd had to interact with extra politeness, which would have formally made this visit a part of the trip. Li began to feel sorry for Zhu, who had to come home often to see his father, while this was the only time Li would ever be there. Who knew how much grief he received from his father each time he was back? It dawned on

Li why, instead of moving to the provincial capital with his son, the old man had remained in the countryside. Zhu was obviously afraid that his father could cause him a great loss of face. Li congratulated himself on the productive trip while gloating over Zhu's unenviable situation, when the old man spoke up again:

"I'll help you out, so now you have to do something for me."

"What is it?" Li was slightly taken aback.

"I have a grandson on my sister's side who works in the county courthouse. He's been there five years and wants a promotion to section chief, but it hasn't happened. They're discriminating against us, don't you think?" He then pointed at the county party secretary.

"And he's the worst. I've talked to him many times about this, but it's always in one ear and out the other."

The party secretary's face reddened again. Li knew that something else was going on when he saw the other cadres exchange glances.

"Don't you worry, Gramps. I'll look into it later."

The old man was relentless. "Later means never. I need an answer from you now. Will you do it or won't you?"

Feeling himself cornered, Li was irked but amused, so he clapped his hands and said, "I'll give you an answer now, Gramps. I'll take care of it."

"You're a provincial official, so you can't go back on your word."

Li grasped the old man's hands and said, "A gentleman is as good as his word, Gramps."

Finally, the old man smiled. "Now, at last, I can see."

"What can you see?" Li wondered aloud.

"That you and Yuchen really are good friends."

That was exactly what Li wanted to hear. He hoped the old man would pass the positive energy on to his son. No matter how bad the blood had been between him and Zhu, coming to see Zhu's father on his own initiative and taking care of what the old man wanted should mean that Li was conceding and admitting defeat. He hoped Zhu would sense his goodwill, which would in turn rouse his conscience enough to move their relationship in a positive direction. As they left the Zhu house, Li had Yu ride with him, as usual, but he also invited the party secretary to take the passenger seat up front. Yu spoke up the moment the car started moving:

"I tried to talk you out of coming, but you insisted. See the trouble you got yourself into now?"

Once again, Yu only knew half of the story. Li smiled and asked the party secretary about the old man's grandson and his courthouse job. The man just shook his head and sighed over the county's misfortune of having a leader with such a father. His grandson did indeed work at the county courthouse, but he was not too smart and was in fact barely literate. That didn't matter as much as his temper, which mirrored the old man's. It took little for him to argue with his colleagues. When the chief judge criticized him, he had the nerve to smash the man's cup. He saw other people getting promotions and wanted one himself. A courthouse section chief is the head of an adjudication section. If he were to assume a position like that, who knows how many erroneous judgments he would pass down?"

"How about transferring him out of the courthouse?" Li said. "For example, a section chief at the farm machinery bureau?"

The party secretary heaved another sigh.

"I thought of that long ago, but he's a bully and wants to stay at the courthouse because of the power. That's why it's so hard."

That cleared it up somewhat for Li, who then asked:

"Besides trying cases, aren't there other positions at that rank?"

"Yes, there's office manager. But the whole court would be thrown into chaos if he had that job."

"How about a logistics position?'

"Every unit has a fixed number of posts and ranks. You can't make a cook a section chief, can you?" The man shook his head.

"Of course not, but can't we set up a logistics section chief?" Li proposed. "He would have the same rank, but his job would be shopping for provisions at the market. If he wanted to get into an argument, he could do so there."

Yu Deshui clapped his hands in agreement after a momentary silence.

"Great idea. We create a new path."

"It's like the Jade Emperor trying to pacify the Monkey King by sending him to feed horses with the newly created title of 'Equine Tender,'" he added.

"That's a good idea," the party secretary agreed. "It satisfies the bully's vanity while taking him out of the courthouse. Killing two birds with one stone." He too clapped his hands and said, "I'll get the position created and add a quota for that rank at the courthouse." Then he slapped his thigh, "Why didn't I think of that? I've suffered the old man's tirades for more than a year."

"Every rank has its own level of intelligence," Yu said. "If you'd reached that level, you'd be governor, wouldn't you?"

The three of them had a good laugh over that, after which Yu invited Li to dinner in the city. He accepted the invitation, since there was nothing important waiting at his office. But then his cell phone rang. He answered it and listened for ten seconds before saying, "I see."

He put his phone away and said to Yu that the call was from the general office. A meeting had been called for that night, so he had to return to the capital. Yu nodded. Li told the driver to pull over, and the cars following them stopped. Everyone got out, and Li shook hands with all. Then the two cars carrying Li and his staff turned onto the highway and sped toward the capital.

3

The call had not been from the provincial government, nor was there a meeting that evening. It was Li's wife, who told him that something had happened to their son, and that he must hurry home. Their seventeen-year-old son, Li Dongliang, literally meaning pillar, was a high-school sophomore. At nearly six feet tall, he had a physique like his name but was a poor student, failing every subject. He was built to fight and never shied away from using brute force; all the boys in school feared him, and even the hooligans around the campus showed him respect. That was why those who caused trouble at other schools did not dare to do the same at his. He had caused his father considerable grief over his frequent fights, leading to a great many beatings. Once when he was exhausted from beating his son, Li asked him why he was like that.

"I was born at the wrong time," the boy said with a sigh.

"What do you mean?"

"If I'd been born in the Song dynasty, I'd have gone up to Mount Liang to join the resistance against corrupt officials like you."

Li gave him a backhanded slap. "What the fuck do you know?"

Every family has its troubles. Zhu Yuchen had an exasperating father; Li Anbang had a troublemaker for a son. When he got the call from his wife about another incident with his boy, he lied about the meeting because Yu Deshui and the county party secretary were in the car with him. After saying goodbye to them, he placed a call to his wife.

"Whom did he fight this time?"

"Not a fight," his wife said. "He was in a traffic accident."

His hair stood on end. "Is he alright?"

"He's fine except for a gash on his head."

He was relieved.

"Whose car was it? How could they be so careless?"

"He was trying to avoid a newly dug ditch when his car skidded off the road and hit an excavator." She added, "It's the city's fault, with its nonstop roadwork."

Ignoring her complaint, he demanded angrily, "Who lent him a car this time?"

At seventeen, Li Dongliang was not permitted to drive. Yet with an executive vice-governor for a father, many businessmen befriended him, despite the age difference, and sometimes lent him their cars. To be sure, that occurred behind his father's back, although Li knew about it. Now, however, he'd had an accident.

"Serves him right. This time I'm not only going to beat him, I'm also going after whoever lent him the car," Li said.

"Now is not the time to do that. It gets worse." She was choking up.

"What do you mean?"

"Dongliang is fine, but not who was riding with him."

"Who's that?"

"A woman."

"Who's the woman?"

"I don't know."

"What happened to her?"

"She was flung out of the car."

Li's head nearly exploded. "Is she alright?"

"We don't know yet. They've taken her to the hospital. I'm going there now."

Li told the driver to speed up. As they raced back to the capital, he felt his rage rising, but, after a brief consideration of the situation, he realized that this was no time to be angry. He picked up his phone and called Duan Xiaotie, a deputy head of the provincial public security bureau. Twenty-five years earlier, when Li was a county party secretary, Duan was a policeman responsible for guarding his office. Li could tell that Duan was honest and trustworthy, with a good brain, so he decided to mentor the young man. Wherever Li went, Duan followed, getting promoted from an ordinary policeman to a station chief, to deputy head of the county public security bureau and then its head; from there he was promoted to deputy head of the city public security bureau, and later its head, eventually being elevated as deputy director of the provincial public security bureau. Duan knew how to repay favors. Even in his current post, he continued the custom established twenty-five years earlier, by saluting Li when they met even before a word was exchanged. He was in charge of several areas in the bureau, including the traffic control office, which dealt with traffic accidents. The moment the call went through, Duan Xiaotie said:

"I'm at the scene already, Sir."

His mind now at ease, Li said:

"Let's make this a quick call. I'm on my way back to the capital. Come see me in my office in two hours."

Duan was waiting for Li at the entrance two hours later, when he reached the government building. They went up to the second floor, into Li's office, and shut the door.

"It doesn't look good, Sir." Duan said.

Li stared at Duan, who continued:

"They tried to save the girl, but it didn't work. She died in the hospital."

Again, Li's head nearly exploded. A traffic accident was one thing, but it was another matter altogether when someone died. Li began to stammer.

"How, how could she die? They were in the same car, and Dongliang is fine."

"Dongliang was wearing a seat belt, but she wasn't. She hit a tree when she was flung out of the car."

Li slowly sat down. He had quit smoking years before, but now he took the cigarette Duan offered him, lit it, and took a drag before asking, "Who was she?"

"I told the public security people to check. A call girl," Duan replied in a low voice.

Another shock for Li.

"What? He's already hooking up with call girls?" He continued, "It wasn't at night either?"

"She wasn't just a call girl; she was flung out, naked from the waist down."

"That bastard. What was he thinking?" Li screamed in rage. "Where's that little bastard?"

Duan naturally knew that the bastard was Dongliang. "He's detained, charged under traffic and public safety laws."

Li nodded to show his approval.

"Do you know where the woman was from?"

"Not yet. We need time to look into it."

Li sank into deep thought. When he finished the cigarette, he looked up and glanced at Duan with a sigh. "What terrible timing."

Duan knew what Li meant, and said, "Everyone knows this is a critical time for you. If the media heard about this, there would surely be an uproar."

"Not just the media. I'm afraid it will be subject to manipulation. Just think, someone died. This is serious."

Duan gave that comment some thought before saying, "How's this? We'll change the name of the person who caused the accident."

"What do you mean?"

"She's dead anyway. So, instead of naming the driver as Li Dongliang, we'll call him something else."

Li did not respond to the suggestion, but, after a moment's thought, knew it was a good idea. And yet he was worried,

"Is that safe? What if word leaks out? We don't want to end up with something worse."

"I cordoned off the area with police tape. They're the only ones who know," Duan said before adding, "Everyone who dealt with the accident has my utmost trust."

"Can you find a safe replacement?"

"A living person won't work. We have to find someone who no longer exists."

Li saw what he meant, but there was more he needed to know.

"Can you work out the technical details?"

"Technical investigations and resident registry are both under my jurisdiction," Duan replied.

Li breathed a sigh of relief as he asked Duan for another cigarette. The relief was not about his son, but about Duan, who proved to be well worth his mentoring and help over the past twenty-five years. After finishing the second cigarette, he said to Duan:

"Make sure you find the deceased's family and give them some money." He added, "Any issue that can be resolved using *renminbi*, the people's money, is an internal conflict among the people."

His meaning was not lost on Duan, who nodded and said:

"There's something else."

"What is it?"

"Your wife fainted when she went to the hospital and learned about the woman's death."

That came as a shock. "Is she all right?"

"They gave her a shot for her heart, and she came to. She's a patient in the hospital herself."

"Let her stay there," Li said after thinking it over. "That way she won't cause us any trouble."

His intention was clear to Duan, who nodded again.

Li had more for the young man, "What we just talked about, don't breathe a word to her."

Duan nodded a third time.

4

Li Anbang's wife was named Kang Shuping. With a peasant background and no connections, Li had attended an agricultural college thirty-five years earlier. With a degree in farm machinery in hand, upon graduation he was sent as a technician to a farm equipment station in Kang Family Shop. Besides earning him a pair of eyeglasses, four years of college had taken him from one village to another. Old Kang, who ran a general store in town, had three daughters; the first one unfortunately looked like him, while the second one had similar bad luck by taking after his wife. The third girl, Shuping, resembled neither parent; she had thick brows over large eyes, a tall, slender figure, and a lovely face. Townspeople wondered about her origin. It was still fashionable for girls in the countryside to sport braids at the time. Kang Shuping had nice, thick hair that she turned into a large braid that hung all the way down to her buttocks. Even dogs stopped and cocked their heads to look at her when she walked from one end of the town to the other. Being a smoker at the time, Li Anbang often bought cigarettes at Old Kang's store. His favorite was Flying Horse, which, at twenty *fen* a pack, was relatively cheap but had better tobacco and fewer stems than other brands in that price range. Those would pop when smoked. Growing up in the countryside and being assigned to work there, Li had thought he'd spend his whole life at Kang Family Shop. Back then, few college graduates came to work in the countryside, and Li was the only one at Kang Family Shop. He and Kang got married after someone made the match for the "talented young man" and the "pretty girl." After the wedding, Li realized that, despite looks that did not match her parents, she shared a habit of theirs—frugality. She could make a square of fermented bean curd last two meals. At a time when Li could only afford Flying Horse cigarettes, it was a laudable trait to be industrious and thrifty in running a household. The two of them enjoyed a happy marriage in Kang Family Shop, with only one thing that marred their contentment—she could not give him a baby. After they both had checkups at the county hospital, they learned that she had been born with a partially blocked fallopian tube. Over the following eighteen years, she ingested all sorts of Western and Chinese herbal medicines, until at the age of thirty-nine, she finally bore him a son. By then Li had been promoted to the position of vice mayor—the former farm equipment technician who had spent his days visiting villages and peasants and dealing with tractors and water pumps had never imagined he would be an official one day. The times produce their heroes. Back during his third year at the station, the central government had issued a document stressing the need for intellectual and youthful infusion into leadership levels, stressing that every county's leadership team must have at least one member under the age of thirty, a college-educated individual with grass-roots work experience. After a county-wide search, Li turned out to be the only qualified individual and embarked on a meteoric rise, from a mere technician to the deputy county chief in charge of agriculture. Later he was promoted to be the deputy county party secretary, county chief, county party secretary, vice-mayor, and on up to his current position. Thinking back, he felt the sharp turn in his career was like a dream. Even now he still dreamed about Kang Family Shop. In one recurrent scene, he is repairing a pump at a village well when the county party secretary barges in and says:

"Another document has arrived from the central government. 'Li Anbang's promotion to deputy county chief has been rescinded.'"

Li tugged at the man's lapel and sobbed.

"How can that be, Secretary Meng, now that I finally got to be the deputy county chief?"

Meng pointed at the pump and said:

"See, see. Aren't you a technician again?"

Looking down at his grease-stained hands, Li would be startled awake. It would then take him a while to recover. As he moved up again and again, Kang Shuping followed him from the village to the county, to the city and eventually to the provincial capital, where he realized that her laudable trait was slowly turning into a flaw, for they no longer needed to practice frugality. Not only did he earn enough to support the family, he also no longer needed to spend his wages, for he was constantly getting gifts of rice or local specialties from the fifteen towns and counties under his jurisdiction. Then there were people in charge of more than thirty department committees who also sent daily necessities and food items to him all the time. With gifts from various channels, it was more than they could possibly consume. Li's taste in cigarettes had experienced a similar hike, from Flying Horse to Zhonghua. Such a lifestyle took some getting used to for him, let alone his wife. Now that they did not have to be thrifty, she stopped being frugal. Her scrimping habit took on a new form: she would take anything they could not use or eat to sell at a shop and collect the proceeds. In addition, she shared her father's habit of record keeping. She wrote down every gift in a notebook, including the names of the senders. Sometimes she would flip through her notebook at night and say:

"Are you having trouble with so-and-so?"

"Why do you ask?"

"It's been a long time since he gave us anything."

Li didn't know whether to laugh or cry.

"It's common practice to bring a gift when they come to see us. There's no requirement that they do so."

"Then why is this guy here all the time? You have to agree there's a difference in your relationships with some people." She didn't buy his argument.

"I'll be in trouble if you keep this up," Li said with a look at her notebook. "No sweat if nothing goes wrong, but if it does and I come under investigation, everything you wrote here would be turned into evidence against me.

"Your father kept an account of the stuff he sold to others. What you're doing now is keeping a record against me," he added.

She had to agree, so she tossed the notebook into the fire the next morning. Watching it curl into ashes, he said:

"You've done the right thing."

"I have an account book in my head. I don't need a notebook."

Sure enough, three months later, she was still able to give him a list of who had sent what over those three months. She did not miss an item, be it an old hen or a basket of salted duck eggs; she also remembered who failed to show up with gifts. Li had to laugh despite his annoyance. As he moved up the official ladder from a county official to executive vice-governor, the ranks of the gift-givers rose as well, as did the gifts. Li realized that she stopped talking to him about the gifts and started dealing with them on her own, even behind his back. When he'd worked at the municipal level, those who dealt with her and called her Big Sister were county chiefs, county party secretaries, or proprietors. After he became the vice-governor, those who dealt with her and called her Big

Sister now were mayors, municipal party secretaries, and businessmen in the capital; they sought to curry favor with her, sometimes with gifts, sometimes marketable securities, and sometimes just plain cash. She would then help them on Li's behalf. When he found out, he gave her a tongue-lashing. Once he even slapped her, saying it was not the same as taking an old hen or salted duck eggs back when he was the deputy county chief. He would end up in jail one day if she continued to take advantage of his position and receive bribes; he went so far as threatening to divorce her. She denied that she had taken any marketable securities and cash, while covering her face and saying:

"You wouldn't dare divorce me, Li Anbang."

"And why is that? I'll go to the courthouse tomorrow if I want to."

"If you do, I'll tell people what you've done all these years. I have an account book in my head, and I know what you've done."

She turned and walked off, leaving Li in a mixed state of amusement and irritation. He had thought his woman was just petty, but it turned out that she was calculating where major issues were concerned. In the meantime, he loathed those men in various leadership positions and the businessmen who hung around her all the time. They gave her small favors so she would help them with matters they could not handle themselves, and in the end, they were the ones who benefitted. They liked the fact that she was not very bright, calling her "Big Sister" as if they were family, but they were in fact taking advantage of her low intelligence. As the saying goes, you should check out its owner before you hit a dog. When they exploited Kang Shuping, didn't that amount to taking advantage of Li Anbang? But that was his wife, whose mindset remained confined to the grocery store at Kang Family Shop, even though she was now the wife of the executive vice-governor. What could Li do about that?

Then there was their disappointing son, Dongliang. Kang was thirty-nine when she had the boy. Having a son at such a late stage had led her to spoiling him in every possible way. Before he turned four, she never took him to the toilet; instead she helped him relieve himself in their living room. Once, when he was five, he peed on her neck when he was riding on her shoulders. He giggled over his act; so did she. When he was six, he wanted a toy car, even though he had over forty of them already. She refused and he secretly shat in her shoes. She raised her hand to hit him when she found out; he did not cry, but she did. After starting school, he was always getting into fights. Each time he got into trouble, she would go to school to smooth things over for him. Even when he turned fourteen, she still cradled him at night and sent her husband to another bed. Li tried to explain to her many times how she would lead to their son's ruin if she continued to spoil him like that. Sometimes he would sigh and say:

"He's not your enemy, so why are you trying to destroy him?"

"You have no right to criticize me. Besides sleeping in your bed, you don't even spend an hour at home each day. Have you fulfilled your responsibilities as his father? I'm leaving him in your hands starting tomorrow. You can take him to school."

That shut him up. She was not being unreasonable. When Dongliang was born, Li Anbang was already the vice-mayor, which required him to be away for thirteen or fourteen hours a day, working at the municipal office in the day and attending banquets at night. His son was still in bed when he left early in the morning and already asleep when he returned at night. Where would he find the time to check on him? It was not uncommon for father and son to not exchange a single word in a week. Sometimes, he even forgot he had a son, who was only a vague image in his mind. Dongliang was not stupid. He might bully his own mother, but he behaved himself when Li was around, never acting up or running wild. Sometimes a mere frown on Li's face would make him shake from fear, and his mother would wrap her arms around him and scold Li:

"Don't bring your frustrations home with you."

Li was a mayor when his son started school, after which he was promoted to municipal party secretary, then vice-governor, and then executive vice-governor, with an even busier schedule. Sometimes when he inspected the schools and ran into Dongliang's principal, he would inquire after his son's performance. Principals naturally knew they had to butter up someone like Li, so they all said he was a good student with fine character, though he could be naughty occasionally. Boys with the personality of a log will never amount to anything when they grow up, they would say, or everyone who has excelled in his field was a wild, unconventional child. Comments like that usually elicited laughter from those around. It also gave Li the false impression that his son was not perfect, but he was a good boy in general. He never imagined that Dongliang could be an arrogant bully at school and could care less about his studies. He had been a troublemaker at both the municipal and provincial schools, and now he was hooking up with call girls and even causing a death. Li's first reaction when he heard that his wife had fainted at the hospital was:

"Serves you right. I told you so, but you wouldn't listen."

Then his loathing turned to everyone who had come into contact with his son—the businessmen and minor officials, as well the principals and teachers at the schools Dongliang had attended. It was they, working hand in hand with Kang Shuping, who had pushed his son to this state. Then his thoughts took a different turn: his wife may have been detestable, her and the toadies, but he too had to bear some responsibility. All these years, he had been singularly focused on his work and forgot to teach his own child the ways of life. It was a father's fault when a son did not learn to do the right thing. His son getting into such serious trouble at this critical moment in Li's career had to be considered retribution.

But Li also knew that the more serious the trouble, the more he needed to keep a cool head, and the more he had to act as if nothing had happened. His wife would not nag him now that she was in the hospital, and his mind was put at ease by the way Duan Xiaotie was handling Dongliang's accident with the dead call girl. He showed up at the provincial government office punctually the following day. In the morning, Governor Ju called a meeting to examine issues of developing the western mountain area, attracting outside investment, alleviating poverty, relocating residents in a reservoir area, and so on. That same afternoon, Li took the heads of the city's urban construction department to inspect two sites in the east. The capital was building its very first subway, which fell under Li's control as well. Be it at the office meeting in the morning or at the construction sites in the afternoon, Li spoke up when needed and gave instructions when they were called for, without showing any sign that something was amiss. He even had a minor argument over resident relocation with Xi, the vice-governor in charge of reservoirs, which led the governor to step in with a joking comment:

"It's understandable that Old Xi is conservative with resident relocation. He visits the area often, and I hear he even has a mother-in-law there."

That made everyone laugh. Yet Li continued to feel unsettled all day, even though he had spoken up, inspected, and given orders whenever necessary. A dead body that could be traced to him was lying in the hospital morgue, after all. He did not sleep a wink that night. But when dawn arrived, he followed his daily schedule, this time taking people to a certain city to inspect its containment of environmental pollution. The day after that he went to another city to look into its progress in improving the slums. It was late in the day when they were done. On the way back in the car, he received a text message from Duan Xiaotie:

Turned into dark smoke/the smoke is gone/the clouds have left

Li breathed a great sigh of relief. Turned into dark smoke meant the woman at the morgue had been cremated; the second phrase meant that an agreement had been reached with her family, proof that the culprit in the traffic accident no longer existed in the world. When someone did not exist, no one would try to find him, for there would never be a record. After quitting smoking for eight years, he had smoked two cigarettes with Duan three days earlier, and now he asked for one from his secretary, who was in the passenger seat up front. He lit it, took a long drag, and exhaled deeply. It was not just the accident that had vanished like smoke and dispersed like clouds but also the negative impact on Li's candidacy for governor. Another text arrived:

Would like to meet/report on something else

Nothing could be worth worrying about when compared with his son's accident and the woman's death. His mood greatly improved, Li phoned Duan.

"Let's have dinner tonight. I'll fetch a bottle of thirty-year-old Maotai from home."

His secretary remarked when he put away his phone:

"I don't see the governor this happy very often."

"An old schoolmate just got here from Guangzhou," Li said with a laugh. "He got me drunk the last time I was in Guangzhou. Now he's in our territory, and I must get even."

"Should I arrange for a place?" The secretary picked up his phone.

"It's a personal get-together. You don't have to worry about it," Li said before adding, "This man has a multinational business. We don't have to spend our own money when the capitalist pays. That can be considered getting the rich to pay for the poor."

Both the secretary and the driver laughed.

5

Li Anbang and Duan Xiaotie were to meet for dinner at a diner called "Xue's River Cuisine." When they were back in the city, he got out of the car in front of his building and sent the secretary and the driver home, saying his friend would send a car for him. He went upstairs, took a shower, and changed into a casual outfit before rooting out a bottle of thirty-year-old Maotai and wrapping it in a sheet of newspaper. He walked out and hailed a taxi.

Duan was waiting outside the diner when he got there. A small place like this was his usual spot for a private dinner with Duan or with his staff. Small eateries usually stayed open until three or four in the morning, as the owners worked hard to make a living while providing a convenient service to those on late shift or anyone craving a snack. In years past, as executive vice-governor, Li had had dinner engagements at high-end restaurants, when extravagant meals were in vogue. He could never get used to lavish banquets that cost 10,000 yuan or more per table, probably because of his rural background. Fancy food at the banquets, like abalone, sharks' fin, swallows' nests, sea cucumbers, and geoducks smelled gamey and fishy to him, and he had to force himself to pick up a few morsels with his chopsticks. In the meantime, he thought it was a veritable crime to spend 10,000 yuan or more on a meal, for it was what a peasant family would make after toiling in the field for a whole year. A diner for the common folks, like Xue's River Cuisine, was his choice for a good meal, which would cost under 50 yuan for two people. Restaurants for the common folk used lots of oil in their cooking and never scrimped on condiments, so the food was salty and spicy, with strong flavors. The food matched Li's taste perfectly. In recent years the central government had "eight rules," prohibiting officials from indulging in food and drink, which came as a liberation to Li. Granted, as the executive vice-governor, he was often on the TV news, so sometimes he was spotted at small diners with a crowd of various types. More often than not, the other diners did not know who he was; they came to eat, not to see famous officials, after all. If he did not make a big deal of his presence, no one would pay him any attention. Even if occasionally someone knew who he was, they would only be impressed by his lack of official airs and willingness to be among the people, surprised that an executive vice-governor would eat at a place like that. The most he would get from them was:

"Are you here to see how we're doing, Governor Li?"

"You have a higher political awareness than I do. I'm here to eat, but you're making it work-related," Li would say.

That would usually make everyone laugh. The daring ones would come up and ask for a photo with him, and he'd oblige. A meal like that revitalized and put him in a cheerful mood, which was the best possible outcome. Li and Duan walked in and sat at a corner table near the river. Duan called over the owner's wife and ordered two cold dishes —peanuts boiled in salt water and smashed cucumber salad—plus four cooked dishes—quick-fried pork with dark sauce, fried smelts, Mapo tofu, and quick-fried shredded potatoes. All Li's favorites. This was not his first visit to the diner, and the owner's wife recognized him. She found nothing remarkable about seeing him again; instead, she asked as she took their order:

"I hear they're building a new road by the river, Governor Li. Will it affect our house?"

Li knew the city's construction department had planned to revamp the riverside, with a park in the center of the river to turn it into a local scenic spot, cultural highlight, and tourist site, which would outshine New York City at night when all the buildings along the river were lit up.

"We're working on the plan and haven't settled on anything yet," he replied with a smile. "I don't know if it will affect your house, but if it does, I promise I'll find you an even better spot along the river."

She breathed a deep sigh.

"Amitabha. I can sleep well tonight after what you said. I've been losing sleep over this for two weeks now."

"I'm doing it for myself, not for you. Where would I go to eat if your river cuisine were gone?"

Laughing heartily, she ran happily to the kitchen and came out two minutes later with the two cold dishes before returning to cook the four. After getting them two large beer steins, Duan took a look around to make sure no one was watching before removing the newspaper around the bottle of thirty-year-old Maotai Li had handed him. He uncapped it, poured the contents into the steins, and put the bottle into his satchel, partly because he did not want the other diners to see it since they could only afford liquor that cost 12 yuan a bottle. In addition, pouring a bottle of liquor into two large mugs was a habit of theirs developed twenty-five years earlier, when Duan drank with Li, who was county party secretary at the time, someone who worked day and night. Sometimes Li would sleep in his office when he did not feel like going home after working into the night. They had not had a child yet, and his wife was working hard on it, in fact trying every night, which taxed him. He stayed in his office and worked until midnight, when he would feel hungry. There was usually another man awake in the county office compound, and that would be Duan Xiaotie, the policeman guarding the building. Li would call Duan over and give him money to buy a roasted chicken or a cooked goose at the street corner, as well telling the young man to roast some peanuts on a brazier. Li would bring a bottle of liquor out of the bedroom, get two large mugs, and divide the contents equally between them. They then tore off pieces of the chicken or goose, shelled the roasted peanuts, and drank until they finished everything half an hour later. In the beginning, Duan did not dare try the liquor.

"I'm on duty, Secretary Li, I can't drink. I'll eat peanuts to accompany you."

"What are you on duty for?" Li asked.

"To ensure the party committee's security."

"A county would be in turmoil if its party committee isn't safe, and there could only be two possible reasons why that would happen."

"What are they?" Duan scratched his head.

"One, the Japs come and seize control of our county, and two, the masses rise up to topple the Communist Party. Do you think either one of those might happen now?"

"No," Duan said after a brief consideration.

"You must be on guard if you think it might, but drink up if you think it won't."

Duan took up his mug. "You're right, Secretary Li," he said with a hearty laugh. I'll drink with you, but please don't tell the bureau chief tomorrow."

"You have my word."

They picked up their steins and drank, not expecting that they would still be drinking by the river in the capital city, after twenty-five years had passed in the blink of an eye. But things were different now. Li was executive vice-governor and Duan was deputy director of the provincial public security bureau. Li would say emotionally sometimes when he thought back:

"It was so much better twenty-five years ago, now that I think about it."

"I've never had as good chicken or goose as back then."

"I don't mean those," Li said.

Duan looked at Li, who replied:

"We were so young. Nothing is better than youth."

"You look quite young to me, Sir."

Li shook his head with smile.

On this day, they looked at the lights reflected in the water as they drank and ate the peanuts and cucumber. Soon the owner's wife brought out the four hot dishes. Li took another sip after a bite of the pork.

"Your text said you want to talk about something else. What is it?"

Duan stopped eating. "First things first, Big Sister has to leave the hospital right away."

He meant Kang Shuping, of course.

"Isn't it better to have her stay there? That way she can't mess things up."

"She hasn't done that, but something else is up."

"What do you mean?" Li froze.

"She called me every hour a few days ago to ask about Dongliang and the dead woman. Not wanting to alarm her, I didn't tell her he was arrested; I told her he was in a safe, secret place. And I didn't tell her much about the woman either, except to say I would take care of it and she shouldn't worry. She stopped worrying and calling me once she knew everything was fine. At the time I thought it was better to keep her at the hospital and out of the complicated situation. Then Mr. Qi, the head of the hospital, called me this morning to say she should leave as soon as possible."

"What do you mean?" Li was stunned.

"She fell ill over Dongliang's accident, and now that everything was fine with him, she's fine too. Once she recovered, she started calling people, and now everyone knows where she is. Starting the day before yesterday, a string of people began going there to see her, mostly businessmen, but also a few city officials, with so many presents they're piled high in her room. Mr. Qi said, "By flouting the "eight rules," she's doing something that others may use against you at this critical juncture. Mr. Qi is with us on this. That's why he told me."

That was unexpected. He hadn't visited his wife since her hospitalization. First of all, Duan had been there dealing with the traffic death, and Li did not want to draw attention to himself. Secondly, his wife was doing well after she regained consciousness, so there was no need for concern. Thirdly, he had to go about his daily work as usual so no one would detect anything. Lastly, he had been too much on edge to worry about her, while the traffic accident and the death were being secretly managed. He had not anticipated that, left alone for a few days, she would cause trouble behind his back again. He'd wanted her to stay there so she would not stir up anything, only to be told that she was creating an even bigger mess in her hospital room.

"That stupid woman is going to be my ruin!" he said through his teeth.

He had felt like banging the table, but he managed to control himself when he saw that the diner was full. Instead, he said softly:

"Go give her a scare. Tell her the provincial commission for inspecting discipline has started an investigation on the gifts and that if she knows what's good for her, she'll leave the hospital immediately."

Duan nodded to show he understood.

"And the second thing?" Li asked.

"Dongliang must leave the city immediately too."

Another surprise.

"I thought everything was cleared up, like smoke dissipating and clouds dispersing."

"I'm not worried about other people. It's him I'm worried about."

"What about him?"

"It's his mouth."

Li looked at Duan for him to continue.

"He's been behaving badly at the detention center. They've treated him with kid gloves, putting him in a room by himself, with two dishes at each meal. But he wants more, asking his guards for cigarettes and alcohol. Whoever heard of someone smoking and drinking in a detention center? The policeman rebuked him and guess what he said?"

"What did he say?" Li asked.

"I'll deal with you bastards when I get out."

Li lost self-control this time and slammed his fist on the table, drawing the attention of the other diners. He tried to cover it up by pretending to get Duan to drink, "It's your turn. Don't try to get out of it."

Duan picked up his stein and took a big gulp before lowering his voice. "He's scheduled to be released tomorrow, according to the detention warrant. I'm afraid he'll be indiscreet and blab it all over. Maybe he won't, but it's hard to say after he has something to drink. He likes to brag, and if he treats this as a heroic feat and crows about it, Sir, you'd —it's a human life, not a small matter."

"Just like his mother. He has no sense." Li seethed, before adding with a sigh, "But where can we send him?"

"The farther the better."

Li thought long and hard.

"Keep the bastard locked up for two more weeks."

Duan realized that keeping the boy in detention was not merely to keep him from causing trouble but also to prevent him from stirring up anything worse over the next two weeks, a critical period for Li. If something bad were to happen, it would not be the boy who suffered.

"I'll think of something when I return and get the paperwork done." Duan added, "But we can't keep him there forever. We have to come up with a long-term solution."

Li nodded. Losing interest in food after learning the two news items, he signaled for Duan to pay up at the counter. He wanted to go home early to gather his thoughts and find a long-term plan to deal with his son. It occurred to him that it would have been just fine if his wife's fallopian tubes had been fully, not partially blocked, and there had been no way to fix the problem. If that had been the case, the evil spawn would not have been born. He sighed and picked up his jacket. Duan returned from paying when he was about to leave.

"There's something else I need to tell you, Sir."

Draping the jacket over the back of his chair, Li sat down again.

"What is it?"

"A personal matter."

"What kind of personal matter?"

Duan stammered as he replied:

"I know there'll be changes in the provincial government leadership. Based on the usual pattern, a municipal leadership shift will soon follow. I wonder if you could help me, Sir, so I can gain experience working down there."

"How would you do that? You're deputy director of the provincial public security department. You can't be demoted to a municipal role."

"I want to leave the public security sector and become a mayor," he stammered, "like Song Yaowu."

Song Yaowu was another man Li had mentored. When Li was county party secretary, Song was the commission secretary. Like Duan before him, Song was a man of few words but had a good brain and knew how to draw inference about other cases from a single instance; he carried out tasks on his own without boasting. Li promoted the loyal, principled young man as deputy office director, after which he was sent to a village to be its party secretary. Li transferred him three years later to be a deputy county chief. As Li's career took off, so did Song's, moving all the way up to a mayoral position the year before. Like Duan, Song stood when he spoke to Li, even after becoming mayor, calling him "Governor Li" when people were around and "Old Leader" when they were alone. But Duan Xiaotie and Song Yaowu were different. Song was cultured and brainy, and, after serving as a party official at the village, county, and municipal levels, logically moved up the ranks and became a mayor. Duan Xiaotie, in contrast, had only been a policeman with limited education. Granted, he had benefitted from a series of promotions in the public security realm —county, municipal, and provincial—they were all subsidiary leadership positions, and it would be unprecedented for him to cross from that to a supervisory position, such as the mayor of a city. Li frowned and said:

"My word carries weight in some areas, but municipal party positions need the consent of the provincial party secretary and the governor. I have no say in this."

"You will, Sir, once you become governor," Duan said with a smile.

That comment put Li on alert, for Duan had been talking about Li's wife and son before bringing up the request. By dealing with the traffic accident and the woman's death over the past few days, he had created a link between Li's promotion and the accident, speaking of them in the same breath. This sounded almost like a form of blackmail to Li, whose promotion would be affected if his son's accident and the woman's death were exposed. If he became governor, it would have been due to Duan's feat of pulling off the deception, and Li would have to repay kindness with kindness. He now saw Duan Xiaotie in a different light.

"I've never heard you mention changing posts. Did you come up with the idea or did someone give you the notion?"

"How could I have discussed a matter like this with anyone? It may sound half-cocked, but it's my own," Duan said, leaving no room for doubt.

Li knew that was not true, but Duan was so new to this that Li easily sniffed him out.

"It's good that you're thinking like this. It means you want to keep improving," Li said without revealing his real thoughts.

"That's what I figured. Staying in public security all my life is too limiting."

"How long have we known each other, Xiaotie?"

"Twenty-five years," Duan replied. "I was your guard when you were the county party secretary."

"Have I done some things for you over that time?"

"I couldn't have been where I am today without your support and patronage."

"And do you think I'll keep helping you?"

"Of course, you will. All central government leaders employ their own people," Duan said firmly.

"There's more to it than that. What do you think that might be?" Li said with a shake of his head.

Baffled, Duan could not come up with anything.

"Because you've been helping me all along, too," he said. "You assume that I can only help you as governor. But I'm saying I could recommend you to the party secretary and the governor even if I didn't get the promotion."

Duan was greatly moved. "Thank you again, Sir," he replied.

Li touched his finger to his lips to remind Duan of the diners around them. Duan blanched and smiled bashfully. Li picked up his jacket and walked out ahead of Duan.

6

Li could not find a good place to stash his son after thinking about it all night. He agreed with Duan that Dongliang would cause trouble sooner or later if he stayed in the city after his release from the detention center. And that trouble could turn into a big mess. The following two weeks would be critical for Li. Who could let them keep his son locked up, but after that, what? He couldn't keep the boy locked up for the rest of his life, could he? He knew he had to find a long-term solution. To be sure, he could send his son away to attend school in Beijing or some other province. In his position, Li frequently went to Beijing for meetings and to other provinces to exchange ideas; in other words, he knew officials in many places and had even become good friends with some of them.

But if his son could cause trouble in his province, who could guarantee that he would act differently elsewhere? If Dongliang acted up away from home, he would be too far away for Li to do anything about it, and that would be a huge headache. It seemed more feasible to keep his son close, so he could wipe his ass if necessary.

After tossing and turning all night, Li still could not find a virtual cage to contain the animal that was his son. He'd have no trouble finding a cage with steel bars if it were a real animal. But his son was human, and an animal to boot. To be sure, a human can be locked up in a detention center or prison, but it was hard to find a usable cage while he roamed freely in society, a man-made cage for which a reliable gatekeeper is necessary. Where would he find such a cage and gatekeeper? He thought until his head hurt. Was there a safe place anywhere in China's vast territory? He sighed. His ancestors obviously had not amassed enough good karma to keep the heavens from sending an evil spawn to destroy him. Or maybe he owed his son something from their previous lives, and now the boy had come to exact payment. The sleepless night had made his eyes puffy.

As he was being driven to the office, he looked out the backseat window and felt that everyone was happier and luckier than he was. Even a worker, a migrant laborer, or the owner of a small diner offering "river cuisine" could be happy with simple food and weak tea, so long as he had a good wife and forward-looking children. But not Li Anbang. He might be a provincial leader, with power and status, but at home he had a befuddled wife and an unruly son who had caused a woman's death. His son was nonchalant about the trouble he stirred up and the possibility that its consequences might implicate his own father. As these thoughts swirled in his head, Li's car reached the government building, whose entrance was guarded by soldiers. They knew his license plate by heart and saluted when they saw it drive up.

That salute gave him an inspiration: wouldn't sending his son to the military solve everything? For one thing, strict military discipline would rein in Dongliang, and for another, soldiers were not allowed off base without a good reason, so the boy would not have a chance to stir up trouble. The military was like a sealed barrel, which meant Dongliang would be hidden from view. As the saying goes, you can wear out metal-soled shoes looking for something and in the end might land on it without even trying. Li's mood brightened as the road opened up before him. He placed a call to an army commander surnamed Liao as soon as he was in his office. Li and Liao had met and become friends six years earlier, when he was party secretary in the city where Liao was the army commander. Over major holidays, Li visited the army base as a representative of the municipal party committee, and Liao reciprocated by visiting Li, which brought the two men close.

Liao was on the short side and had a booming voice, like a large bell. When he laughed, he could make a room quake with his echo. Besides a loud voice, he was also endowed with a large capacity for alcohol and outdrank Li, whose village and county stints had giving him plenty of experience on the liquor battlefield. Li had allotted the army an extra hundred acres when Liao was enlarging the base, for which the commander was enormously grateful. When the Yangtze River flooded one year, Liao stationed a division and a mechanized brigade along the levee to ensure that the river did not breech its banks. The amicable relationship between the city and the army base became a much-told story in the area. The Ministry of Civil Affairs had honored the city as a "Model Supporter of the Military," while Liao's soldiers were commended as "Model Supporters of the Government and the People." Before Li left the city for his new post as vice-governor, Liao hosted a private banquet for him at the base. When the dinner got underway, Liao said:

"As a token of my appreciation, today's dinner will not cost the public anything." He added, "The military and the people are family. Here, I'll drink three cups first."

After downing those three cups, he continued, "Brothers are closer than anything. Here, I'll drink six cups."

Then Li stood up and drank nine cups in a row. Getting drunk midway through the meal, they draped their arms around each other and began to weep. Li would feel reassured by placing his son in the military, especially in the hands of a friend like Liao. So, he dialed Liao's number. Two rings later Liao's thundering voice nearly burst Li's eardrums:

"You screwed up, Governor Li."

"What do you mean?"

"Now that you're being promoted to be the governor, you can ignore us common folk. You were in town last week and didn't stop by. Isn't that a case of bureaucratism?"

Li laughed.

"Don't listen to gossip, Commander Liao. I'll consider myself lucky if I do a decent job in my current position. I spent only half a day there," he added, "and I didn't want to disturb you. I'll make a special visit one day soon."

"Do you have something for me to do? Deputy War Zone Commander Qin is here to inspect our combat readiness, and I have to accompany him to visit the mechanized brigade. Can you make it short?"

Li complied.

"You've met my son. He idolizes you and would like to be a soldier under your command. Will you take him?"

Liao laughed.

"Of course. I welcome him with all my heart. How old is he?"

"Eighteen." Li added a year.

"Why isn't he off to college?"

"Isn't the PLA a college too?"

Liao laughed again. "Let me guess, if you don't mind my being direct. Is he not doing well in school?"

"You always go right to the heart of the matter, Commander Liao. He's a bit wild, which is why I want to send him to you."

"We're experts with wild kids," Liao said. "Quite a few of the provincial and city leaders send their boys to us because they can't get into a college, hoping for entry into a military academy, an indirect route. Is that what you have in mind?"

So there was another venue besides being a soldier, Li was surprised to learn. His plan for Dongliang would amount to killing two birds with one stone, if the boy eventually got into a military academy. Taking the lead handed to him, he said, "I'll rely on Commander Liao to take care of a problem I can't solve."

More laughter from Liao. "A look at the headquarters compound reminds me of Governor Li. You did me a big favor, so I'm happy to run errands for you."

"Can I have him report to duty next month?"

Liao hesitated. "I'm afraid not. He'll have to wait until the recruiting season to join. Those are the rules. The Central Military Commission has been very strict about this." He continued, "August is recruiting period. It's April, only four months from now." Then he added, "Why are you in such a hurry, Governor Li?"

Li could not press his case after a response like that, for it would arouse suspicions over his motive.

"No hurry, no hurry at all. Thank you, Commander Liao. We'll wait till August."

Li's conundrum hung on. It was an ideal route, but they had to wait four months. Dongliang was still at the detention center. How was he going to get through the period? He could not keep his son there that long. As he stressed out over the situation, his office director came in to say a peasant and a young man were outside the building, demanding to see Li. The guards tried to shoo them away, but they refused to leave. The old man said he was Li's uncle. Li thought it might be a country bumpkin from his village or his wife's hometown, Kang Family Shop. People like that were not sensible and would refuse to leave if he did not meet them. Sometimes they became unreasonable and caused an uproar, exploiting their peasant background. With a frown, he said, "Send them in."

Li was surprised when the old man and his young charge entered his office. It was none other than the father of Zhu Yuchen. A few days earlier, he had used an indirect method to ease the eighteen-year rift between him and Zhu by going to visit the old man. Then Dongliang had a traffic accident and killed a woman, which was so serious a matter that Li was preoccupied and completely forgot about Zhu's father. He never imagined that the old man would show up at his office a mere few days later. Li was recovering from the surprise when the old man stormed over, grabbed his hand, and shook it hard.

"You're the best in the whole word, dear nephew!"

Li was flabbergasted, not knowing what the man was referring to. The younger man came up to tug at Li's sleeve.

"One word from you, Uncle, and the county courthouse found a solution for me. I'm going to be the head of logistics."

Now Li recalled. Back at the village, the old man had made a request about his grandson, who worked at the county courthouse and wanted to be a section chief. Li had said he would go back to think it over, to which the old man had accused him of being shifty and demanded a straight answer on the spot. Cornered, Li had promised to take care of it. On the way back, he'd talked it over with the party secretary Yu Deshui and his county counterpart, finding a solution by installing the young man as logistics chief. Li had not expected them to get into action right away; they'd taken care of it within a few days. He then noticed that on the floor behind the two men were a basket of chicken eggs, several cases of soft drinks, a few bottles of liquor, and several cartons of cigarettes. They were there to thank him.

"I'm glad it's been taken care of," he said. "Are you happy with your position?"

"I couldn't be happier, Uncle. I work at the courthouse, but I never liked dealing with lawsuits. I've always been interested in finance."

"Now he's in control of everything they drink and eat," said the old man.

Five days earlier, when they were in the car talking about creating the position, the county party secretary had remarked that the young man was not reliable and a bit dimwitted. After listening to him, Li realized it was an accurate assessment. The two of them, young and old, talked back and forth, a perfect pair in their lack of common sense. Even so, the old man was Zhu's father, and Li was desperate to patch up the rift with Zhu. Put differently, a word from Zhu, good or bad, could determine if Li became governor or not. The local cadres had also revealed that Zhu was still afraid of his father even now; once the old man had slapped him in front of some people. Having a good relationship with the old man would be like controlling the emperor to order the dukes around in feudal times. Buoyed by the thought, Li told his secretary to make tea and extended a lunch invitation to the pair. The old man accepted it unceremoniously, and held up his thumb, "You're very sensible, nephew."

"What do you mean, Gramps?"

"When I tell people back home you invited us to lunch, our status will go sky-high."

Li simply did not know whether to laugh or cry when the young man said, "When I go back, I'm going to tell everyone at the courthouse that I had lunch with the governor. Now we'll see who dares do anything to me."

Li told his secretary to order a business lunch at the government dining hall. He had another dilemma. Now that the old man was in town and he had invited them to lunch, he wondered if he should notify Zhu, whose office was across the street. He did not have to, but this was Zhu's father, and Li had tried to get on the old man's good side in order to improve his relationship with Zhu; the opportunity was enhanced by the fact that Zhu feared his father and did not fear Li. He could let Zhu know, to be sure. But they had been on the outs so long that it would be awkward to try to smooth things over with a lunch invitation. It would make his objective too obvious, wouldn't it? Caught in a bind, he could not make up his mind, so he changed tactics by asking the old man:

"Does Director Zhu know you're here, Gramps?"

"I came to see you, not him. Why should I tell him?" The old man pointed at Li and continued, "You're more efficient than him."

Li knew what the old man meant. He continued to probe:

"Do you think we ought to invite him to lunch?"

"This is between you and me. Why ask him?"

Li decided against telling Zhu. A look at his watch told him it was only ten-thirty, so he had his secretary take the pair to rest in the reception room, while he stayed to do some paperwork. At noon, he got up to go over to the dining hall, but paused outside his office to tell his secretary to notify Zhu's secretary, who would then notify Zhu that his father was in town and would be having lunch with Li. He was welcome to join them if he could get away. After giving the matter much thought, Li had decided not to lose the opportunity for a face-to-face reconciliation. The central inspection team would be arriving in five days, and time waits for no man. Unsure of Zhu's reaction, he did not want to blunder by being overly clever, so he had his secretary talk to Zhu's secretary, easing the possible pressure on Zhu by taking an indirect route. When he reached the dining hall and entered the reserved room, the visitors were waiting for him. He offered them tea, which they drank until a server brought in cold dishes; no word from Zhu Yuchen's office. After a look at Li, his secretary came up and murmured, "Should I call Director Zhu's secretary to see if I can urge a response?"

Li raised a hand to stop him from making the call. Zhu was not a child, and eighteen years of enmity could not be erased by a call and a meal alone. He'd come if he wanted to and if not, no call would get him over; in fact, Li could end up looking overeager. Instead, he turned his attention to his visitors.

"Let's begin, Gramps. Want a drink?"

"We don't get to see each other often, so of course I do."

Li smiled as he told his secretary to uncap the bottle. The visitors were not shy and, after three toasts from Li, started toasting each other, drinking up a storm. Li got up to use the toilet and ran into Director Ji of the provincial department of education, he grabbed Li's hand. "Do me a favor, Governor Li."

"What's that?"

"Visitors from the Ministry of Education are having lunch in Room 208. Please come meet them."

"You should ask Vice-Governor Bai, who's in charge of education maters."

"Yesterday Governor Bai left to check something out of town and got stuck in traffic on the way back this morning. It'll be a serious lack of decorum if they're not greeted by someone of your rank."

"Who are they?" Li asked.

"No one very high up actually. A departmental deputy director-general and a section chief. But they deal with the renovation of condemned elementary and middle school buildings, with a budget of billions. As the saying goes, a turnip may be small, but it grows high on the ridge, not in the field. If you greet them, we may get several hundred more buildings for our schools. With a stroke of their pen, they can give us tens of millions. For the sake of our children, Governor Li—"

"Say no more. I'll go." Li could not refuse after what the man said, but he added, "I have to be straight with you. I can't stay long because I have my own important visitors."

"Sure, no problem. A brief hello will do." Old Ji thanked him.

After relieving themselves, Li followed Ji to Room 208, where he greeted the officials from the Ministry of Education. As it was an official reception, no alcohol was served; using tea as a substitute, Li toasted them and exchanged some pleasantries before returning to his own reserved room. He discovered that, while he was away, his visitors were red in the face from alcohol and were slurring their speech. They did in fact come across as unsophisticated people who behaved the same no matter where they were. He knew he must not let them drink any more, for if they caused a scene, they would not be the only ones who looked bad. Li would further alienate Zhu Yuchen if he learned that Li had gotten his father drunk. So, he signaled his secretary to end the banquet. At that moment, the door opened to reveal Zhu Yuchen. His face dark, Zhu walked in and, ignoring Li, looked at the table and at his father and nephew, whose red faces showed the effects of alcohol. The visitors jumped to their feet when they saw Zhu, who pulled out a chair and sat down. The look on his face made them tremble, as they remained standing. Li knew at once that the rumor about Zhu's fear of his father was false, and it was utter nonsense that Zhu's father had ever given Zhu a slap out of anger. In fact, Zhu's father was afraid of his son, not the other way around. When the rumored relationship was turned right side up, Li was able to match the Zhu before him with the one from twenty-five years before. Someone who had started out as a county party secretary and made it to the rank of provincial cadre would not fear a grimy old country butcher. It dawned on Li why the old man would not tell his son about his trip to the city. Maybe he originated the rumor about Zhu's fear of his father. He was actually frightened of his son and had lied to puff himself up, like draping a tiger skin over himself to intimidate people. He had mentioned to Li what he had not dared bring up with his son, and Li had actually helped him out, which had led to the visit. Seen this way, Li had not put one over on the old man; he was the one who'd been played by falling for the old man's trick. He was tickled despite his annoyance.

"It's not enough that you're a disgrace back home, but you must also come to cause a scandal here, is that it?" Zhu fixed his gaze on his old man before turning to glare at the young man. "I just called the county office and heard about your farce. You're no longer a section chief."

He finished with a shout, "The car is waiting outside. Get yourselves back home now."

Like the demons exposed by the Monkey King's magical club, the pair showed their true colors and sobered up, no longer blustering. They slunk out of the room and vanished. Zhu stood up and turned his gaze on Li. "Disgusting."

He turned, slammed the door, and walked off.

Li fell into a chair once Zhu was gone, keenly aware that he had been too clever for his own good, like a thief failing to steal a chicken and losing a handful of rice in the process. He had hoped to improve his relationship with Zhu through Zhu's father, but his misjudgment of the father-son relationship had led Zhu to misunderstand his effort to help his father. Now Zhu thought Li was mocking him. In his view, Li knew that the demand made by Zhu's father and the dimwitted young man was outrageous, and yet Li had told people to go ahead with it. That could only mean that Li was trying to make a fool of him. Or it could mean that Zhu had intuited the real reason behind Li's action—Li was one of the candidates for the governor's position and the central government was sending an inspection team led by Zhu's old classmate. Instead of being upfront about things, Li had engaged in underhanded maneuvers and, worse yet, had tried to scam Zhu's family members. He obviously felt that Li had treated him like a dimwit, which was why he'd said "disgusting" on his way out. By that, was he referring to the entire incident or to Li's moral character? Either way, Zhu's utterance could only mean a clean break between them. Zhu might not have said anything positive about Li, but he would not likely have killed his hopes either without Li's twisted route to salvage the situation. Now, seeing through Li, Zhu was convinced that Li had played him and his father for suckers, which would only lead to burning all bridges between them. Eighteen years earlier, the position of executive vice-mayor had been enough for Zhu to falsely accuse Li of accepting two million yuan. With new enmity piled on old acrimony, he would likely lie about Li to his classmate and accuse him of accepting as much as two billion yuan, enough to separate his head from his body. Seeing how the blow had dumbfounded Li, his secretary said in an unnatural voice, "Director Zhu is so rude."

That roused Li, who replied, "I did not expect him to misread the situation. I just wanted to help his family out." He shook his head. "Nothing you do is right if someone considers it with bad intentions."

But the consequence was not lost on him, and the more he thought about it, the more frightened he became. He went back to his office and spent the afternoon mulling it over, but he failed to come up with a way to deescalate the situation. And calamities never come alone. His secretary rushed in shortly before he was leaving and gave him more bad news. It was much worse than antagonizing Zhu. According to the secretary, his protégé, Mayor Song Yaowu was under double discipline, ordered by the disciplinary committee to give an account of his wrongdoings at a required time and place. Li was stunned.

"When did that happen?"

"Two hours ago."

"There was no warning."

"That's right. Mayor Song was at a meeting this afternoon and was taken out the back after the meeting ended."

Li slumped in a sofa. The disciplinary committee had to be in possession of ironclad evidence of a cadre's violation of disciplines and the law when it issued a double-discipline order; it would not act rashly to alert the accused. Moreover, no one ever emerged innocent under such a situation because they always confessed to charges of corruption. The committee took its time and gave nothing away when conducting an investigation, so no one was aware of anything going on. But once it had sufficient proof and the time was right, it sprang into action and launched an attack. Oftentimes, someone could be a guest on a TV show and disappear the day after, followed by an announcement on the committee's website that so-and-so was under double discipline. In the past, Li had been impressed by the committee's work when it happened to someone out of the blue, for he'd been far removed from the occurrence. But now with Song Yaowu being the target, it felt like a disaster lurking around the corner, for Li had been Song's mentor and had helped the young man at every step. During the process of helping Song reach where he was, some exchanges of favors had surely taken place, which had happened not over one or two but twenty-five years. Over that time, Song had assumed many roles and served as a senior city and county official; if the exchanges were discovered, it would be enough to send Li to jail, if not the chopping block. That Song was being investigated was an irreversible fact; what worried Li now was whether Song would implicate others. Historically, Li knew that every guilty cadre gave up names. In many cases, the guilty official confessed to every corrupt act over the decades as soon as he was taken away in the car and before it arrived at the interrogation site, where he'd blab the names of anyone involved in his corruption. If everyone else blabbed, why wouldn't Song do the same? If he did, then it would not be long before Li himself received the same order. He broke out in a cold sweat as Duan Xiaotie opened the door and raced in. In the past, when he came to see Li, Duan had always been announced by the secretary, or at least had knocked first. But today he came in without knocking.

"Song Yaowu, Sir—" He was out of breath.

"He knows." The secretary stopped Duan softly.

Duan Xiaotie and Song Yaowu had met twenty-five years earlier, and Li Anbang had mentored them both. Hence, Li thought they should know each other like brothers. When Li and Duan had had dinner by the river the day before, Duan had used Song as the precedent when he said he wanted to leave the capital to be a mayor. Li wanted to have a private talk with Duan, so he signaled his secretary, who left the room and closed the door behind him. Li turned to Duan. "You know Song Yaowu well. Does he have guts?"

"He's timid as a mouse, which is why I'm so worried." Duan shook his head as he replied.

"How's that?"

"Back when he was the executive vice-mayor, he was involved with a waitress at the city guesthouse and got her pregnant. She wanted him to get a divorce, threatening to post pictures of them in bed on the web. I was the deputy chief of the public security bureau, so he came to me for help. Imagine a grown man crying, with snot flying. In the end I took charge and frightened her into silence, besides offering her 300,000 yuan to abort."

"How come I didn't know about that?" Li said.

"He wouldn't dare breathe a word to you. If a woman could put him in that state, with the disciplinary committee and the means available to them—"

Li felt a chill bore into his heart, but he knew better than to show Duan what he was thinking, for he had discovered at dinner the night before that Duan was a different man. He could trust no one. "I'm aware of what's happening," He said. "You go on now. I need peace and quiet to think."

Duan got up to leave, but hesitated, so Li asked, "Anything else?'

"I think something's going on with Dongliang's traffic accident."

Li was shocked. "Wasn't it taken care of? I thought you'd found a non-existing person."

"I sensed this morning that our department director reopened the case. As the man in charge of traffic control and technical investigations, I dealt with the case, but he reopened it without consulting me. So, I think something is going on."

Li's head nearly exploded.

7

The investigation of Song Yaowu and the reinvestigation conducted secretly by the department head were like two arrows aimed at Li Anbang. He would fall if either of them hit him; it would no longer be a question of whether he would be the next governor, but if he would find himself under double discipline and end up in prison. On the surface, the two events were unrelated, but they might create a domino effect, one leading to the exposure of the other once it was uncovered and resulting in something else. Most fearful was the existence of vile men like Zhu Yuchen, who, upon getting wind of Song's trouble or Li Dongliang's traffic accident, would not likely let it go. He would surely add fuel to the fire and hit Li when he was down, which would amount to a third arrow that might as well be ten thousand of them piercing his heart and sending him straight to the chopping block. He knew he'd made a mortal enemy of Zhu but had no idea how many others were waiting secretly to see him disgraced. During his three decades of government service, he had occupied all the positions that could antagonize someone. Forget about what had happened in the past and look at the present situation: with three candidates picked by the central government for the governorship, they were enemies now even if they had never had issues with each other. Hadn't the rift between Zhu and Li eighteen years earlier also resulted from their both being nominated for the post of executive vice-mayor? Besides, what was at stake now was the governorship, which would carry much more rancor and resentment, and if it could be harnessed as energy, it would be powerful enough to fire nuclear missiles, not just arrows. People these days were different; no longer kind and obliging, they would be pleased to see him fall from grace, instead of recalling what he had done for them.

After not smoking for eight years, Li had smoked a few cigarettes over the past few days. Now with a dark cloud looming over him, he saw he had nothing to lose and told his secretary to get him a pack. Without realizing it, he had smoked all twenty cigarettes when the clock on the wall told him it was one in the morning; he had yet to find a solution to deal with the three arrows. In fact, he did not know how to deal with even one, let alone all three. He would like to discuss it with someone because he was stuck for a way out, but he had not had a friend in years, after the lesson Zhu had given him. At such a critical moment, where would he find a friend? Chairman Mao once wondered in distress: Who can I consult when the country is in peril? Li felt he was in the same position as Chairman Mao.

Failing to produce a name after wracking his brains, he turned on his cell phone to scroll through the list of calls he'd made and received. There were more than a thousand individuals, but not one of them was someone to whom he could bare his soul. He could talk to them about daily life or work, or share perfunctory comments or jokes with them, but he could not tell any of them the trouble and worries he was having. He fully understood what Lu Xun had meant by "Having a single confidant is enough for a lifetime," for one needs such an individual to talk over problems and find solutions, not to share food and drinks or romantic dalliances. But persistent effort sometimes does pay off. After dismissing one thousand and twenty-two unreliable people, he came to number one thousand and twenty-three with the name Zhao Pingfan, and his eyes lit up.

Zhao was a well-known real estate developer from his own province. He had built many commercial buildings in the capital, as well as landmark structures such as the provincial museum, the new provincial gymnasium, the eastern station of the high-speed rail, and a high-tech college town. His commercial structures were found all over. As executive vice-mayor,

Li had been in charge of urban construction and had gotten to know Zhao, who liked to say that he was in the business of simplifying complicated matters. At the time, the city had decided to develop a multiuse plaza that would include sculptures and a musical fountain surrounded by commercial high-rises with shops, restaurants, movie theaters, and an arcade. With a projected budget of two billion yuan, the development had received bids from dozens of developers from many provinces, including Zhao Pingfan. One day Zhao showed up at Li's office and said:

"Give me the plaza project, Mayor Li. The others are all con artists."

"The bidding isn't finished yet, how can you say that?"

"The bid is just a formality, isn't it?"

"It aims to be open, fair, and impartial. How could you say it's a formality?"

Zhao picked up a piece of paper from Li's desk, wrote something, and pushed the paper over to Li. He'd written:

"My final bid will be 200 million yuan."

Li was about to say something when, to his surprise, Zhao picked up the paper, stuffed it into his mouth, chewed it up, and swallowed it.

In the end, Zhao's company won the bid. After assuming the project, he employed the best designers in the country and the best construction company from the province. The work was never shoddy; he shunned inferior material and did not try to speed up the work schedule. When it was completed, the complex was rated as superior construction by the provincial department of housing and urban development, a model for the province. Li then realized that Zhao was a man with vision, someone with whom he could be friends. The two men were in frequent contact after that, and Li, in his capacity as vice-governor and later executive vice-governor, had helped Zhao win the bid to build the new gymnasium and the high-speed rail station. Sure, it was mutually beneficial and, naturally, Li had kept his wife in the dark. Later Zhao shifted the focus of the business to Beijing, where he built several landmark structures. And then in February of the previous year, he had abruptly announced his retirement, just when his career had reached the heights. He moved back to the provincial capital from Beijing. No one, including Li Anbang, understood why. Once when Zhao invited Li out for tea, Li asked him why he'd given up so early.

"I did a calculation," Zhao said.

"Of what?"

"I'm sixty-five now, which means I have two more decades to live, one of them disease-and-disaster-free. I've worked for money all these years, now it's time for money to work for me."

"In what way?"

"So that I can eat and drink what I like and have some fun."

Zhao was an extraordinary man. From a certain perspective, he could be considered optimistic, sensible, and insightful. With their mutually beneficial past, his retirement meant a safe landing for Li in regard to their exchange of favors. Li could now breathe a sigh of relief. Based on what he read online, Zhao's personal worth was over three hundred billion yuan when he retired. The two had met less frequently since Zhao's retirement, and Li had learned from others that Zhao traveled the world to play golf, ski, paraglide, climb the Himalayas, and visit the South Pole. When they did meet, it was under very different circumstances, such as after a national disaster, like an earthquake, a drought, or a flood, or when the provincial government planned to build a nursing home or set up funds for the poor; that brought Zhao out with his donations of a million yuan, five million yuan, even 100 million yuan. He gave 500 million yuan to the government's planned "Hope Primary School" in a poor, mountainous area in the southwest. Li was also in charge of charitable and public welfare projects and publicly thanked Zhao on behalf of the provincial government.

"I donate money not to be praised publicly, Governor Li," Zhao had said with a shake of his head. "I do it because I have more money than I can spend in a lifetime. Money is a worldly possession, not something we bring with us when we were born or take with us when we die. I grew up poor, so I know who this money can help."

His simple, direct answer won for him loud applause from those in the audience. Zhao's various donations were another sign of his long view, in Li's eyes, as he knew to wash his trail with money. On this night, when Li saw Zhao's name on his call list, he sensed that Zhao was indeed someone he could talk to about the three possible arrows. For one thing, with the favors they'd exchanged, they knew each other's past well, so he could be honest with Zhao. Secondly, with Zhao now in retirement and away from the land of troubles, Li could talk to him about his problem. Thirdly, from the way he washed his trail with money, Li knew the man was sensible, with a clear understanding of broad principles. He very likely could offer some ideas. Urgent matters cannot wait, but the clock on the wall said it was almost two in the morning. Zhao could be asleep, his cell phone turned off, he could be away from the capital city, he could be in another city, even overseas. Li decided to send him a text first.

"Where are you? Asleep?"

Zhao responded in less a minute. "At home. What can I do for you?"

The heavens will always create new roads. Li was elated as he dialed the number, "I can't sleep, Old Zhao. Let's go for a drink?"

"Come on over," Zhao said with a laugh. "I just received a shipment of Australian lobsters, live ones, of course."

Li gave the suggestion some thought before replying, "Let's go to Xue's River Cuisine." He added, "Don't forget to bring a bottle."

Li left the office, hailed a taxi, and went to the river. Zhao was waiting by the door when he got there. It was where Li had had eaten with Duan Xiaotie the day before. At two in the morning, only a few tables were occupied, two of them by loudmouthed drunks. The owner's wife was dozing at the counter, her eyes bloodshot from a lack of sleep, but they lit up when she saw Li walk in. "Back so soon, Governor Li? You were here yesterday."

"It's the food," he said. "People are like dogs when it comes to food, always going back to the same place." He added, "We'll have the same as yesterday."

She nodded and cast a glance at the clock on the wall. "It's hard being governor; it's after midnight and you're still working."

"For me only today, but you have to stay up every night till three or four in the morning," Li replied.

"You really don't put on airs, Governor." She laughed. "And you're always thinking about us."

She raced back to the kitchen cheerfully, as Li and Zhao sat down at a corner table. Zhao had invited Li out to diners like this before. Years ago, when Zhao was given the high-speed rail east station project, they had worked out the details at a similar place. Knowing Li's dining habits, Zhao went to get two large beer steins before retrieving from his satchel a bottle wrapped in newspaper. After a look around to make sure no one was watching, he removed a bottle of thirty-year-old Maotai, uncapped it, poured the contents into the steins, and put the empty bottle back into his satchel. By then, the owner's wife had brought out two cold dishes—peanuts boiled in salt water and smashed cucumber salad. With the clink of their steins, they each took a drink before Zhao said, "You asked to see me so late at night, so it must be something very serious."

Li nodded. He turned to stare at the light reflected on the river to collect his thoughts before giving Zhao the details about the three arrows, their origins and impacts, leaving nothing out. At some point in his explanation, he had to stop and exchange small talk with the owner's wife when she brought out the four cooked dishes—quick-fried pork with dark sauce, fried smelts, Mapo tofu, and quick-fried shredded potatoes.

He continued after she left. Zhao kept sucking in cold air as he listened, and spoke up after Li finished, "This is very serious, Sir."

"It sure is. I'm under attack from all sides."

Zhao glanced at the loud drunks and whispered, "Something this serious, we should talk about it at my house."

"It's safer here." Li shook his head.

Knowing what Li was getting at, Zhao nodded his agreement.

"I asked you here to give me some ideas and help me out of this jam."

"The only solution is to go to three separate places to eliminate the potential troubles," Zhao said as he looked at the lights flickering in the water. "Go see the discipline committee about Song and tell them you have had nothing to do with him. For Dongliang's accident, go see the director of public security and stop him from reopening the case. As for Zhu Yuchen ruining your chance, you go and ask him to forget your previous acrimony. But you can't do any of these, can you?" Zhao sighed with a shake of his head, "When it comes to this, you can only trust the heavens and hope for the best. No one can do anything about it."

Li found the comment disappointing, but on second thought, he agreed that Zhao had a point. He too heaved a sigh. Not interested in drinking, they looked at the lights in the middle of the river for a while before Zhao spoke up again, "I don't have a solution, but I know someone who does."

"Who?" Li tensed.

"Yizong."

"Who's that?"

"An *I Ching* master."

"I don't believe in esoteric things." Li was deflated.

"But he has helped quite a few people."

"Like who?"

"Like me. He helped me out once."

"In what way?"

"I had a major setback last year, and a friend suggested that I go see him. He gave me a great idea, which I followed, and then I retired. And nothing has happened to me since. Otherwise, I'd have been in prison this year."

Li was astounded. Was this the true reason behind Zhao's retirement the year before, as well as an explanation of Zhao's washing his trail with money?

"What setback was that? How come I didn't know about it?"

"I offended someone I should have stayed clear of in a business deal." Zhao pointed his finger up. "I didn't know he was connected to a very powerful man." He shook his head and continued, "I didn't realize until then how ignorant I'd been. Beijing is like deep water; he was a shark and I was just a croaker. He'd open his mouth and I'd be in chunks."

"That sounds terrible. Why didn't you tell me?"

"Because it was beyond terrible. Besides, he has a powerful reach, getting you involved wouldn't have helped."

If the man were that powerful, Li agreed that as an executive vice-governor, he could do nothing to help Zhao.

"What did this man Yizong do for you?"

"I promised him I wouldn't tell, that I'd take what he said to the grave."

With a response like that, Li could not pursue the matter. At the same time, he thought that the *I Ching* master must have real talent if he could help Zhao out of something that serious. But Li was dubious. "How can I hand my fate over to a fortuneteller?"

"Call it fortunetelling if you want, but it can also be considered a matter of causality. We humans don't have a total grasp of the unknown. Yizong explained to me the causal links of world affairs and how they're connected. It's actually quite complicated." Zhao added, "You can write it off to any port in a storm. What other options are there?"

This last comment was very persuasive. Having grown up in a rural area, Li was familiar with the popular view that not believing in deities is fine until someone in your family is sick. He was now a political patient suffering from a late-stage disease, beyond the help of standard hospital procedures, so he had to turn to folk remedies. Li made up his mind to pay Yizong a visit.

"Keep this between us," he said as they were walking out of the diner, "what we talked about just now—"

"You don't have to tell me that. Helping you, Sir, is helping myself."

"How's that?"

"With our association, would I stay at large if you were taken in?"

So true, Li thought, sure he'd made the right move to go to Zhao.

8

Li Anbang went with Zhao Pingfan to Yizong's Taoist study early the next morning. Out of caution, they did not take either man's car; instead, they hailed a taxi by People's Park, where the city's residents performed their morning exercises. As Yizong was an *I Ching* master, Li had thought his place must be secreted deep in the mountains or among old growth trees, or at the very least, in the suburbs—any place with natural scenery. He did not expect to find it next to a farmer's market in a residential district in the city's old town. The taxi wove through the lanes, skirted the market, and entered a street lined with vendors' stands where vegetables, fruits, goldfish, noodles, wontons, teppanyaki, and so on were sold. He heard a vendor hawking his wares when they walked into Yizong's yard: "Steaming hot sticky rice cakes!"

It was a building in a traditional compound with three rooms in the middle and two on each side, around a neat yard laid with dark gray tiles.

Three sticks of incense were burning in an incense burner in the middle of the yard. A middle-aged man, gaunt, dressed in a Chinese-style jacket, and sporting a goatee, was tending flowers from a watering can.

"This is Master Yizong." Zhao made the introduction.

"Sorry to trouble you, Master," Li said with his hands clasped.

Yizong put down the watering can to return the greeting with the same gesture. "You are too kind. It's you who has made the trip to deliver business to my door. All visitors are here to feed and clothe me."

They laughed, as another vendor shouted from outside, "Candied fruits!"

Even that made them laugh.

"So Master does not turn down human sustenance," Li remarked.

"As the saying goes, a major hermit can live among the people, while a minor one must be in the hills among the trees," said Zhao.

"Hermits or not, it's all a lie," Yizong said with a wave of his hand. "Reaching enlightenment has nothing to do with a place. Living on simple food and water in a dark alley bothered average people, but Yan Hui, Confucius' disciple, enjoyed it. It is normal to be bothered, but to enjoy it means you've reached enlightenment."

That sounded profound to Li, who nodded as they went indoors, where a stick of sandalwood incense burned in a holder on a table. A pretty teenaged girl poured tea and then walked out. Yizong refilled their cups when they finished.

"May I ask, Sir, what have you come to see me about?"

"He has encountered some setbacks and seeks a solution," Zhao replied.

Yizong brought over a piece of blank paper and picked up a pen.

"Do you mind telling me your birth date, time, and place?"

"So Master uses numbers too?" Li said.

"Oh, yes, but I come up with colors, while others get birth signs."

"What do you mean?" Li was puzzled.

"Oh, I forgot to you tell," Zhao cut in. "Master differs from other *I Ching* masters by summoning up the world in the colors of the rainbow; he's a color master."

That confused Li. "Can you really sum up the whole world in seven colors?"

"Based on the date and time of one's birth, the seven colors interact, seven times seven producing forty-nine hues. Adding in the place of one's birth, with its specific external environment and weather conditions produces further interactions, which makes forty-nine times seven. Altogether there are billions of variations."

Unable to understand a word of what the master said, Li could not tell if he was for real or was putting on a show. But Zhao had said this man had helped him out of a jam the year before, and since it had worked for him, maybe this color business made sense. How could he get anything done if he doubted the man before even starting? He told the man his date, time, and place of birth, which Yizong wrote down on the paper before carrying out a calculation with his fingers. He wrote some more and went back to his finger work. Then he brought out a pile of thread-bound books, removed one of them, flipped through it, and wrote again. He repeated the process more than a dozen times, filling one sheet of paper and starting in on another. Half an hour later he had filled three sheets with dense writing; he went back and forth between the sheets before looking up to say, "I am going to start with your setback, and I'll keep going if I get it right. If I don't, it means I haven't mastered the art and have wasted your time."

"Please go ahead, Master."

"You have a red violation," Yizong said.

"What does that mean?" Li asked.

"It's the worst kind."

Li could only scratch his head.

"Let me start with your status. You're a high-ranking official. Now your setback: you have red cap troubles and are under attack from all sides."

Li was impressed but began to wonder if Zhao had told Yizong about his current difficulties beforehand, giving Yizong something to talk about. On second thought, he knew that Zhao was a sensible man with personal interests intertwined with his own, which meant they would both suffer if one of them went down. Zhao had even said the night before that he would not be at large if Li were taken in. At such a critical moment, why would Zhao try to deceive him? Then another suspicion crept up: Yizong might have seen Li on TV and knew that he was the executive vice-governor, who could only be asking about his official position when he came with a setback. He looked around but failed to see a TV in the room. Sensing what was on his mind, Zhao said:

"Master Yizong never watches TV or uses the Internet. He can't tell you a single name of the members of the Central Committee. He did not know who you were before we came."

Li was still not convinced.

"Master said I have a red-cap problem. Is red associated with government officials?"

"It's not my invention. As everyone knows, colors are closely linked with political bloodlines."

The explanation was lost on Li. "Please be clearer, Master."

"Here's an example. Tell me the eight banners of the Qing court."

"There are the yellow banner, the white banner, the red banner, the blue banner—" Zhao replied for Li.

"Those are political powers divided by colors, aren't they? Even within the same color, there are further divisions, such as the pure yellow banner, the yellow-edged banner, and so on." He continued: "And what about what one wears? Who wore yellow? Only the emperor, right? Court officials' ranks were distinguished by the colors of their robes.

"But let's forget about imperial times and examine your political party. During the revolution, it called itself the red army and the enemy the white army, did it not? We also talk about red power and white terror, don't we?" He added, "At present, the world has political entities that call themselves the blue camp or the green camp, the red-shirt or yellow-shirt army. When a country is toppled, we use color to refer to it as some kind of revolution. The flags of the countries in the world all have their distinct color combinations, too."

Put this way, colors were indeed closely linked with politics, but to Li it all sounded far-fetched. Noting the doubtful look, Yizong took up one of the sheets and said, "Let's put aside your recent setback for the moment. Based on the changes of the myriad colors, I can start with your early life. You had a red violation as early as the age of nine."

That sounded like utter nonsense to Li. A nine-year-old child can have no political ties. He'd been in primary school at nine and wasn't even a class monitor. His doubts did not go unnoticed by Yizong, who said, "Politics is only one of the possible red violations I mentioned. There are all kinds of reds in the world. Think back carefully and tell me about the fire that year."

Li abruptly recalled that he had gone with his maternal uncle to the county seat that year to sell onions over the winter break. They'd spent a night at a roadside inn that had caught on fire at midnight. His uncle had grabbed his money pouch and run out with the others, leaving Li fast asleep inside. In the end, it was the innkeeper who ran in to bring him out and save him from immolation. After that, his parents would have nothing to do with his uncle's family. Li was finally fully and wholeheartedly convinced.

"You're right, Master. It did happen."

Yizong continued to flip through the sheets. "The secret codes of one's life are hidden in colors, but I won't give you all the details, since life would lose its meaning if I did."

"Let's not worry about the distant future, Master," Zhao said. "What's happening now is key. What can be done to resolve my friend's red violation?"

Bringing over another blank sheet of paper, Yizong calculated with his fingers again, after which he wrote something. Once again, he repeated the procedure many times, until after seven or eight rounds, he had filled the sheet with writing, which he read carefully and against the previous three sheets. Finally, he said pensively, "Your problem can still be resolved, but you have only four days. After that everything will be lost."

He was impressed. The inspection team would arrive in four days.

"Please tell us how, Master," Zhao said, "since time waits for no one."

Yizong was lost in thought as he scanned the sheets before replying, "There are ten different resolutions for most matters, but there's only one for this particular problem of yours."

Li looked unnerved as Zhao persisted, "What should we do?"

"I can't tell you," Yizong said with a sigh. "It's immoral."

"Please rest assured, Master, that whatever you tell us today stays between us," Zhao said.

Yizong kept quiet, prompting Zhao to add, "Let me assure you, Master, that we'll make it worth your while."

"That's not what I meant." The master shook his head, paused, and continued, "Old Zhao and I go way back, so I'm doing this for his sake and will tell you. You can take it or leave it. A red violation must be resolved when you see red."

"How do we do that?" Zhao said.

"Find a virgin."

Li was flabbergasted: the idea that the three arrows could only be blunted by taking a woman's virginity was outlandish. He glanced at Zhao and saw that his friend was similarly dumbfounded.

"Please be clear, Master. What's the connection?" Li asked.

"Have you ever noticed the color on the wall around the Imperial Palace? If you see red, you break down the walls."

Li thought about the walls, which indeed were red. Did he really have to break down this kind of red wall? Ignorant of the interactions between colors, he felt like laughing despite his confusion. But Yizong gathered up the sheets and gently tapped the edge on the table, a sign that the session was ending.

"Please don't be upset with my incessant questions, Master," Li continued. "Let's assume your method works. There are still difficulties involved."

"Like what?"

"Where do you find a virgin these days? You can't go looking for one at a primary school. That's against the law."

"Look carefully. You'll find one without breaking the law," Yizong said.

"Please be clearer, Master," Zhao said.

"I'll say one more thing, even though it's immoral and would shorten my life—old revolutionary, minority, border and poor areas."

He stood up, so did Li and Zhao. From his satchel Zhao took out a stack of money wrapped in newspaper and laid it on the table. Yizong ignored it and came out into the yard, followed by the others. He walked up to the burner and bowed three times before tossing in the sheets, watching them burn to ashes. Then he clasped his hands as a gesture to see them off. As Li and Zhao headed out of the yard, Yizong took the can from the girl and resumed watering the flowers.

Li was the first to speak when they came out onto the street.

"Is he the tight-lipped sort?"

"You can be assured of that," Zhao replied. "He has professional ethics. He forgets what we came to him for once we're out the door. Didn't you see him burn the paper in front of us?" He continued, "Anyone who comes to seek help from him is by definition in a real jam, and all of them are well connected. He wouldn't have survived till now if he had a loose tongue.

"He's the one who told us to keep it quiet. He's even more cautious than us," Zhao added.

"Can we believe all the crazy stuff he said?" Li asked.

"The way things are, we have no choice." Zhao added, "We have nothing to lose if we follow his instructions and they don't work."

Li smiled unhappily. At the end of his rope, he could do nothing but give it a try, like trying to revive a dead horse.

"Let's say we believe him. Where are we going to find the solution? I don't think what he said about seeking virgins in these regions makes much sense. Most of the prostitutes in the city come from poor regions."

"Speaking purely from probability, we still have a better chance in backwaters than in big cities," Zhao offered.

"Even so, these are remote areas, and I'd likely be in jail by the time you found one."

To his surprise, Zhao waved off his concern and said, "No problem. I'll take care of everything."

"What do you mean?"

"I've spent the past year eating, drinking, and enjoying myself. I know who to talk to about this."

9

Deep in the mountains outside the capital city was a traditional residential complex called B18.

It was here the following night where Li took the virginity of a woman.

Before meeting her, Li was concerned that his worries would be too distracting for him to perform in bed, which would mean he would not take her virginity, and that would mean he could not solve his problems. Failing was no big deal, but he'd be in hot water if he could not overcome the crisis, which amounted to a wasted effort in finding the woman. The more he thought about it, the less assured he was, so he decided on some external help. Li had arranged for her to eat and bathe right after she arrived, while he took a Viagra.

10

He performed better than he'd expected.

He not only took her virginity but also had the best sex in five years.

The woman was from the mountains, with cheeks tinged with a high plateau red; she did not really look Chinese, and said her name was Song Caixia.

She was plainspoken and answered all his questions. Her answers sounded believable. She was also sensible, for she never asked his name.

11

Three pieces of news arrived over the next three days.

The first: Mayor Song Yaowu kept his mouth shut after his double discipline. No matter what questions were posed to him, he gave the interrogators the silent treatment, like Zhang Chunqiao of the "Gang of Four." A stalemate developed and went on for two days, but they got nothing out of him. At midnight, he asked to use the toilet and was walked there by the two guards. As he was walking out after finishing his business, he spun around when the guards were not paying attention, pushed open a stall, and rammed his head against the valve on the pipe at the corner, with so much force that he cracked his skull and died on the spot in a pool of his blood.

The guards were punished.

Two: Zhu Yuchen, the deputy director of the provincial People's Congress, had undergone a routine physical exam four days earlier and learned the results the day before. He had late-stage lung cancer. The test results were disclosed in the morning, and by that afternoon his family had sent him to the cancer hospital in Beijing. The advanced stage of the disease created the question of whether an operation was necessary. His wife and children were divided and had an argument.

Zhu had to put his work aside and focus on getting better.

Three: the provincial public security department reopened a misjudged traffic death investigation. A middle-aged businessman had smashed his car into a road repair vehicle; he was unharmed, but the young woman in his car had died on the spot. She was a call girl. The businessman had paid his driver four million yuan to take the blame. The investigation uncovered the truth, and the businessman was arrested. It took only five days to close the case, since Secretary Mao of the provincial commission oversaw the case himself. The head of the provincial public security handled the arrest.

Li could not stop sighing emotionally each time the news came. Duan Xiaotie had once said that Song was a coward, who would surely betray Li once he was under double discipline. Li had not expected him to be such a loyal, upright man who would rather sacrifice himself than sell out a mentor. Song had an aging mother and a wife with a young child, so Li vowed to take care of the family. Zhu Yuchen's diagnosis floored Li. Now that Zhu was dying, he would be focused on staying alive, with no time to wreak havoc on Li's life. No matter how great the rift had been, Li would forget it as long as Zhu did not do anything to his career prospects. Li was determined to attend his old friend's memorial if he died. The reopened case of the traffic death turned out to be nothing at all. Duan Xiaotie had simply overreacted, confusing the two traffic accidents, both involving a car smashing into a road repair vehicle and causing the death of a call girl.

Three days later, the inspection team arrived to examine the three candidates for governor.

Twenty days later, the central government reached a decision: Secretary Mao would be promoted to a position in the central government, and Governor Ju would be his replacement. Li Anbang would be transferred to another province as acting governor, while an executive vice-minister from the central government would be sent down to be acting governor of Li's province. The two acting governors would be given the permanent governorships when their respective provincial People's Congress held the next elections. Deputy Governor Jing would replace Li as executive vice-governor.

This comprised the central government's latest personnel shuffle.

Li was naturally elated to be governor, and being sent to a different province suited him perfectly. For one thing, he was happy to leave the hotbed of troubles after thirty-five years and put a full stop to the interconnected enmities and kindnesses. Secondly, he would take his worthless son with him, removing the young man from his troubles. Once they were in a new place, he would put the bastard in an appropriate cage and send him to the military four months after that. His elation was tainted by self-reproach, however. He had done so many things over the decades to let down the party and the people. Luckily, they were all in the dark about what he had done; only he knew. He vowed to take these incidents as a warning: he would be an upright and uncorrupted official, would work doubly hard, and would help raise the province to a new level. He knew it was a hard-won position, one that would serve to make up for his wrongs. A position traded with blood.

Upon hearing of Li's transfer to another province, Duan Xiaotie expressed his desire to go along. Li agreed but said Duan would have to wait until Li was well settled in the new place. Li added that his wife had wanted to go with him, but he'd also told her to wait. Now that Kang Shuping had to stay behind, Duan could not press his case.

Li was still buried in work the day before he was scheduled to leave for his new post. Governor Ju, the new secretary of the provincial committee, had one last general meeting the night before, dealing with matters related to the turnover. After the meeting was over, Ju said:

"We're all going to new posts within the province, all but Anbang. I'll tell the dining hall to prepare a farewell dinner for tomorrow night."

The other vice-governor concurred, but Li said he would be attending the opening ceremony of Hope Primary School in a remote mountainous area, a roundtrip that was ten hours or more by car, and might not make it back to the capital in time.

"You're leaving the day after tomorrow, so you'll need to get ready. Why don't I send Old Bai to Hope Primary School?" Ju said.

The vice-governor for education was a fitting representative.

"Sure, I'll go," Old Bai said.

Li explained that the Primary School was a public welfare project under his jurisdiction. Public welfare work was always relatively easy in the capital, but it became increasingly harder the farther down the grassroots level one went, for it relied on the good will of local officials. Now that he was leaving, he needed to bid farewell to the city and county comrades in charge of public welfare.

"We won't keep you then, so you can carry out your duties up to the last moment," Governor Ju said.

Li left with his staff the following morning and ran into roadwork right after leaving the city. Still more than eighty kilometers from the county they were headed to at noontime, they decided to stop at a roadside diner called "Happy Farmers," where each had a bowl of noodles with shredded chicken before getting back into the car. As they neared the city line, they saw members of the city leadership waiting by the highway. Zhao Pingfan, who had been invited because of his donation to the project, was already there awaiting Li's arrival. Everyone congratulated Li on his promotion. The municipal party secretary took Li's hand and said:

"Governor Li is leaving our province soon and has made our city the last stop of his investigation and research trip, which can only mean he has a close emotional bond with the people living in the mountains. On behalf of the five million and more residents of the city, I thank you, Governor Li."

Everyone applauded when he finished. Zhao, standing among the others, clapped without revealing their special relationship. But Li pointed him out.

"Manager Zhao is whom you should thank. He's the one who started it all. Without his money, there would be no Hope Primary School here."

They all thanked Zhao, who waved them off and said:

"I didn't do much. It's all due to Governor Li's stellar leadership."

Everyone applauded again. Then they got into their cars and headed into the mountains, driving two hours to the county line, where the county leadership was waiting by the road. After Li got out and shook hands all around, they got back into the cars to continue their journey. Two hours later, they finally arrived at their destination, where the brand-new Hope Primary School rose before their eyes on a flat spot in the center of the village. Beyond the entrance made of red walls and green roof tiles were five rows of classrooms neatly built with dark green stones. Colorful banners adorned the walls around the campus, and a new national flag flapped in the wind on the pole by the entrance. Li's entourage was greeted by a deafening din of gongs and drums from inside and outside the school. Villagers, all dressed in their finest, were crowded alongside the road and applauding. When they entered the schoolyard, they saw several hundred uniformed village children filling the square. A group of seven- and eight-year-old boys and girls came up with red scarves for Li and his party. Then they headed to the podium amid the drums and gongs. Li pulled Zhao closer and whispered:

"Obviously, the unknown exists."

What he meant was not lost on Zhao, who tugged at his red scarf and pointed at the colorful banners on the walls and the red wall and green tiles at the entrance.

"Yizong was right. Our world is made up of many colors."

"Could these all be coincidences?" Li was dubious.

"Even if they are, you're lucky to have them, Sir," Zhao said.

Li whispered again amid the loud gongs and drums:

"Do you know why I'm here today?"

"You feel strongly about our province on the eve of your departure, Sir."

"That's one thing. I also have a wish."

"What is it?"

"If this bears out what Yizong said, then we need to thank the girl. Her name is Song Caixia, and she's from around here." Li added in a low voice, "She was a virgin, after all."

Zhao was puzzled for a moment before he raised his thumb.

"You're a righteous and loyal man, Sir, spreading your gratitude to one individual to everyone in the area." He added, "After hearing what you just said, I've decided to donate two more Hope Primary Schools to the mountain area."

Li gripped Zhao's hand and whispered one more question:

"What did Yizong tell you to help you out of the jam when you ran up against the powerful man?"

Zhao paused before replying:

"I promised to keep it to myself, but now that you've asked a second time, I'll tell you. I had to split myself in halves."

"What do you mean?"

"Giving them half my assets through stocks, worth more than a hundred billion yuan."

"They were that ruthless?"

Zhao nodded, "The type to swallow you up and not spit out the bones."

Li gripped Zhao's hand again. With the gongs and drums continuing, they mounted the podium, where the municipal party secretary invited Li to unveil a plaque and give a speech. Li did both and asked the school to be run well, before announcing that Zhao Pingfan would donate two more Hope Primary Schools to the mountain area, telling everyone to thank him again. Zhao waved them off as loud applause sounded from below.

The following morning, Li got on a plane with an assistant and flew to his new post.

Chapter 3

Everyone You Know

One year went by.

Chapter 4

Yang Kaituo

1

Yang Kaituo was at his nephew's wedding when the Number Three Caihong River Bridge was blown up. Yang had many friends and relatives in the county where he was born, but he refused invitations to their weddings and funerals, an aversion that stemmed from a desire to keep clear of them, but not because he was an unreasonable man. Being the highway bureau chief, he was responsible for the county's road and bridge works, which led these friends and relatives to believe that he had ownership of them all. If you raise a fat pig, you share it with your own and no one else. They pestered him for construction work, despite the fact that he had already done quite a bit for them. Five years earlier, when a minor road connecting two villages was being paved, the price tag for the three-li distance was 500,000 yuan. Yang was used to approving several millions for road or bridge work, so 500,000 yuan to him was like a single hair from a cow, and he handed the strand to a nephew's construction brigade. It took only a month to pave the road, which appeared well done, but three months later, the surface began to buckle here and there, creating potholes, making it worse than the original dirt path. It earned him the villagers' criticism. He asked his cousin, the nephew's father, how much the young man had spent on the roadwork.

"Two hundred thousand yuan," his cousin had said without blinking an eye.

So they'd spent less than half the amount on the job and kept the rest. Yang had to admire their guts, if nothing else. They were masters of corruption. A substantial number of people had been arrested since the central government launched an anti-corruption drive, which conveniently became Yang's excuse to say no to these friends and relatives.

"So you want me to be arrested, is that it?" he would say to those who came to him for construction jobs.

Fully justified in turning them all down, he did so. Yet they still came asking for favors, which was why he did his best to avoid them.

But he had to attend this particular wedding, for the young man was not just another nephew, but the son of his elder sister. Yang had grown up holding on to her proverbial skirts; without her, there would be no Yang Kaituo. He had contracted meningitis at the age of one. Running a high fever in a delirious state, he was at death's door in three days. Back then, large families were common, since the country had yet to implement family planning. There were seven children in his family, and no one cared much if they wound up with one less. An impatient, hot-tempered woman, his mother left him to his own fate in a grass hut. His sister, who was nine at the time, came to check on him three times a day and give him water. He began to recover three days later. If she hadn't come and his fever had not abated, he'd have died of thirst, if nothing else. Being a frail boy, Yang was frequently picked on at school and cried each time. It was his sister again who took care of the bullies. So now when her son was getting married, Yang decided to make an exception and attend the wedding, making her look good by adding a bit of grandeur to the occasion, for the presence of a county bureau chief would elevate the tenor of the wedding. A banquet of more than a dozen tables was laid out in the yard following the ceremony. Being the highest official, Yang was given the seat of honor at the main table, amid the bride's family members, her uncles and brothers. From the groom's side were, besides Yang, two prominent figures—the village head and the accountant. Yang had a maternal cousin who lived in a neighboring county, a place that specialized in labor exports, which meant taking peasants to Africa to build houses and repair railroads. This cousin, a welder at a Botswana construction site who was back on a home visit, was so tanned he could pass for an African. As an overseas returnee, he was given a seat at the main table. The presence of Yang at the table made the bride's rural guests ill at ease; they kept their heads down and held their tongues. The cousin from Africa, not the articulate type, stared at the new house in the compound and read the congratulatory couplets newly pasted on the door. The awkward silence around the table worried the village head, a sociable man, who said:

"This is a day of great joy, Chief Yang. We must liven things up, so the guests won't go home with the impression that we're too snooty for them."

"He's right," the accountant said. "We have to make sure they all have a good time, or it won't be us, but you, Chief Yang, who loses face."

Yang made sure to keep up appearances for his sister's sake.

"You're right. No one is allowed to walk out of this yard if we don't get a few of you drunk."

That made everyone laugh and loosen up. An old man from the bride's side said:

"You deal with important people and major events every day, Chief Yang, while we're all country folk who can't hold our liquor the way you do."

"The way you're talking, Gramps, I'll bet you can. Drinking is like working. Only those with a great capacity have the nerve to say they can't."

More laughter. The village head was getting animated.

"Let's play a drinking game."

"What's the game?" the welder from Botswana asked.

"Whoever starts the game must first drink three cups, and then play the finger-guessing game with everyone at the table. If he wins more than half the time, he's halfway home and all the others at the table must each drink a cup on their own and then toast the winner together three times. If he doesn't pass, he has to drink for each losing round and three more cups as a penalty. How much you drink shows your capacity."

The others went silent when they heard the rules of the game. The village chief turned to the old man.

"I'll start, Old Uncle. You'll be next."

The old man smiled. "I can't, Chief. The stakes are too high, and I'm too old to keep up."

"If you refuse, Old Uncle," the accountant said, "it will look like the bride's family lacks worthy drinkers."

"I'd like to try if that won't offend the leaders and elders," a young man from the bride's side said tentatively, while reaching out for the flagon. The old man poked the youngster's hand with his chopsticks.

"You don't know the rules. The first round must be led by our leader."

"We're all kin here, so there's no leader." Yang turned to the young man. "We'll start with three rounds. The winner will lead off."

The young man looked over at the old man, who smiled but said nothing. So, he engaged Yang in the guessing game, as everyone laughed heartily and craned their necks to watch. When the young man's cell phone rang, he stopped and took out his phone.

"It's rude to make the Chief wait while you answer your call," the village chief said. "I'm adding another rule. Everyone at the table must turn off their cell phones. Anyone whose phone rings has to drink three cups."

Yang took out his phone and turned it off.

"Everyone takes turns leading the game."

The young man turned off his phone, as did the others. They were all in high spirits by now, the lively air drawing guests from other tables to watch.

"Don't make my in-laws drink too much," Yang's sister said. "It will look bad when they go home."

"We haven't even started, so how could they drink too much? We're not short of liquor, are we?"

That drew a round of laughter. Yang shook hands with the young man before starting the game. After three rounds, Yang was declared the winner, to general applause. He took up his cup and drank three times, winning more applause. Now that he'd passed the test, it was the old man's turn, followed by the village chief, and the young man. Their spirits were on the rise as they continued to drink, all praising Yang for not putting on airs. Two hours later, a young man and a middle-aged man from the bride's family fell into a stupor at the table, while the accountant and the welder ran to the toilet, threw up, and failed to return. Yang was getting light-headed and slurred his words, but just as he was about to shout out a number, his driver ran in with his cell phone.

"A call for you, Chief."

"I'm not taking it," Yang said, his tongue thick. "Didn't I say we all turn off our phones? Why is yours still on?"

"It's County Head Du."

Yang partially sobered up at the mention of the county head. With a smile to the table, he took the phone and held it to his ear. An angry curse hit him like a bolt of lightning:

"Yang Kaituo, you dumb fuck!"

Yang was stunned. Ordinarily he'd have realized that something was very wrong to cause Du's anger, but he'd had too much to drink and the opening volley only angered him. A county head may be superior to a bureau chief, but he ought not to curse his subordinate that way. Yang walked away from the table and replied:

"Tell me if something's wrong, Mr. Du, but don't curse me."

"I'll curse you if I want to. And that's not all I'll do. Let me ask you this. Why the fuck did you turn off your cell phone against government rules?"

"See, you cursed again."

"Fuck you. I guess you don't know that Number Three Rainbow Bridge was blown up an hour ago, and that more than two dozen people died."

He continued, "I'm at the scene, while you're there all fucked up!"

Yang nearly passed out, erasing the effects of alcohol. Construction of the county's roads and bridges was his responsibility. He was expected to take charge when there was trouble.

2

The Number Three Rainbow Bridge over the Caihong River had been built five years earlier with a total investment of 680 million yuan. A tributary of the Yangtze, the Caihong River cut across the county west to east, with two bridges spanning it: Number One Bridge was in the eastern part of the county, while Number Two Bridge was in the center. The western region was mountainous, with rugged roads and treacherous rapids, making bridge construction difficult. Additionally, the counties and towns in the region were sparsely populated, owing to modest economic development. As a result, the torrential Caihong posed an insurmountable barrier to people on both banks at this point; the county seat was only twenty kilometers directly across the river, but officials had to travel an additional eighty kilometers to the Number Two Bridge to attend meetings at the county seat. Five years prior, with a third of the cost from the central government, a third from the province, and the last third from the city and county, the Number Three Bridge was finally built under the auspices of the county's highway bureau. The design was turned over to the province's Institute of Architectural Design, and the construction went through a bidding process before an architectural firm from within the province was brought on board. Yang, who had participated in every step of the process, had been the principal official charged with carrying out the plan. On the day the bridge opened to traffic, red banners flapped over the three-kilometer bridge as gongs and drums created a deafening din amid popping firecrackers. The mayor personally cut the ribbon, to loud cheers of villagers on both banks. News of the bridge opening for traffic even made it into provincial newspapers. Before the bridge was in place, villagers rarely traveled to the opposite bank, but now, after five years, they were marrying their children across the river. Towns and counties in the western region, which had been plagued by poverty before the bridge, were now able to truck out their apples, pears, jujubes, chestnuts, and hawthorn berries, making the villages noticeably richer. When Yang went to the western region to inspect the country roads the day before the banquet, he had driven past the bridge, which towered over the river. How could it have been blown up? Who did it? Had the Americans launched a sneak attack or was it a terrorist organization's handiwork? County Head Du had said the explosion caused the death of more than two dozen people. What were they doing on the bridge at that moment? Yang was filled with questions he did not dare ask over the phone; all he knew was that he had quickly sobered up. He rushed out of his sister's house and was driven to the bridge.

Yang was dumbfounded when he got there. The Number Three Bridge no longer stood proudly under a bright sun. It was reduced to rubble, blown apart in the middle. In the rapids beneath were crushed vehicles, trucks and sedans, one of which was still smoking. The rubble on the bridge was also smoking, while chunks of cement continued to fall into the water. At first glance it looked as if war had broken out. Police and ambulance sirens blared incessantly along the highway; on the banks and in the water, soldiers were rescuing survivors, as onlookers gawked, crowding the area. Standing on one end of the bridge, County Head Du was directing the rescue work. When Yang ran up, Du took a look at him and his anger rose up again.

"You would be considered a deserter if this were war time, and I'd have personally put a fucking bullet in your head." He went on, "Smell yourself. You reek of alcohol. Get out of my sight. I'll deal with you later."

Yang timidly walked away to find Director Yu of the County Government Office, "What happened, Director Yu?"

A decent man, Yu quietly told Yang that the bridge had been fine until two hours earlier, when a sixteen-wheeler from a neighboring province drove across, fully loaded with firecrackers. Unexpectedly, the firecrackers began to go off when the truck was halfway across, igniting the main and spare gas tanks and blowing the truck to smithereens. The power from the firecrackers and two gas tanks amounted to a truckload of TNT, enough to blow the bridge in two. At the moment of explosion, there had been more than a dozen vehicles traveling in both directions. A few at the ends managed to stop in time, while six vehicles closest to the truck had plunged into the river. One was a tour bus with more than forty passengers. Twenty-two of them died on the spot, while the injured were on their way to the county hospital; it was impossible to get a definitive number of casualties, and hard to say if the number would rise. Yang was stunned, but managed to say:

"No one could have predicted this. It was an accident." He added, feeling unfairly wronged, "County Head Du was furious at me, but I wasn't driving the firecracker truck."

"You weren't driving, but you're responsible for the bridge," Yu replied. "It's finished and so are you. Who wouldn't be furious if you turned off your cell phone to get drunk?"

Yang knew better than to say any more. Police sirens were coming closer as a row of vehicles roared up and stopped at the bridgehead. One of the doors opened to reveal the mayor himself. County Head Du raced over to greet the man, who stood to watch the rescue work and pass out instructions, before walking up to the smoking crack on the bridge for a closer examination.

"How could a truckload of firecrackers blow up a bridge made of steel and concrete?" he asked dubiously. "Was there a quality control issue during the construction? This wasn't shabby, tofu-dregs work, was it?"

Yang's head nearly exploded. He had not driven the truck, but if there was a problem with quality control leading to shabby work, then he and the highway bureau would be held responsible. He wanted to go up and try to explain, but the mayor had not finished, and Yang could not interrupt, especially not with the mayor surrounded by the county chief and others.

"Who was in charge of bridge construction?" the mayor asked.

Du turned, searched the crowd, and pointed at Yang when he found him.

"Him."

"Was it you?" the mayor asked Yang.

Too startled to answer the mayor's question, Yang could only nod with a foolish grin, the sight of which brought a frown to the mayor's face. He turned to Du and said:

"Form an accident investigation team at once. I want a thorough study of the cause and the quality of the bridge construction."

Du nodded, and the mayor continued:

"With more than twenty deaths, it's a major incident. We must report to the provincial and central government offices." He added, "And don't lie or hide anything in your report. Last year, when a school in another city had a stampede, they did not report the actual number of deaths, and that cost several leadership positions. Consider that a lesson for us."

"Yes, Sir," Du replied.

Trucks from the pontoon force drove up, so the mayor went to shake the hands of the force leader and express his gratitude. The soldiers joined the rescue work, while the mayor got into his car to return to the county seat, followed by his entourage, to visit the injured at the county hospital, accompanied by County Head Du. Having finally recovered his composure and sobered up completely, Yang got into action: he called the highway bureau to tell everyone to stop what they were doing and hurry over to Number Three Bridge to help in rescue work. In the meantime, he told his deputy in charge of finance to make available 300,000 yuan in emergency funds and to meet him at the county hospital with gifts and fresh flowers. He also asked his office director to draft an apology for the bureau to every resident of the county—in case they needed it. When he finished, he got into his car and raced to the county seat. His deputy chief was already there when Yang arrived; the deputy had brought with him a bag of money and a vanload of gifts and fresh flowers. He told Yang that the mayor and the county head had left after their visit. Yang nodded at the information before heading to the office to see the hospital director. Putting a bag containing 300,000 yuan on the man's desk, Yang said:

"Saving lives is the task at hand, Director Sun, so let's not worry about money. We'll front the money for the expenses now and square it away later." He added, "We must contain the number of deaths, no matter what."

"The mayor and the county head have both given us their instructions. We'll do our best. But ten of the thirty-five injured are in critical condition in the ICU. It's hard to say what will happen to them."

Yang grabbed the man's hand.

"This is a critical moment, so please help me out."

He then went with his deputy to see the injured. Yang shook hands with those in the general ward with minor injuries and presented them with gifts and fresh flowers. His next stop was the ICU, where only medical personnel were allowed in to see patients. Yang looked through the window and saw more than a dozen heavily bandaged individuals in two rows of beds. It was getting dark in the corridor. His head emptied of ideas, he did not know what to do next, when his deputy said:

"You've been busy all day, Chief Yang. It's time to go home for some rest." He added, "You can't change what happened, and worrying about it is pointless."

Yang had to agree, so he turned to leave, but had just reached the staircase when a nurse stormed out of the ICU and shouted:

"Hurry, Dr. Li. A patient's heart has stopped."

Yang sank into a chair in the hallway, feeling as if his own heart had stopped. Doctors and nurses ran toward the ICU, prompting him to leap out of the chair and race over to wait for news. Ten minutes later, a gurney emerged with a heavily bandaged figure, adding another to the total number of fatalities. Sinking back into his chair, Yang did not dare leave the hospital; he paced outside the ICU for two hours, when another body was taken out. He had not been this distressed since his parents died years before and could not take a bite of the food his deputy brought him. As the ICU quieted down, he managed to doze off, but he jumped up when his cell phone rang. Worried that it might be County Head Du again, he checked the screen, which displayed his wife's name, a comforting sight. A glance at the window beyond the hallway told him that daytime had arrived and the sun was up. He breathed a sigh of relief when he realized that he'd slept more than four hours in that chair. Obviously, no patient had been taken out of the ICU during that time. Yang thought his wife might have called out of concern for his absence all night, but her thunderous voice exploded when he answered his cell phone:

"Yang Kaituo, you're a dumb fuck!"

Caught completely by surprise, Yang responded in kind:

"What the fuck? Say what you want, but don't curse."

"Cursing you isn't all I'd like to do to you. Let me ask you, why were you smiling?"

Now he was properly baffled.

"Smiling? Not me. I'm at the hospital, as nervous as a jittery monkey. I haven't had any goddamn smile on my face."

"I'm not talking about you smiling at the hospital. I'm talking about you smiling at the scene of the accident yesterday."

That was even more disconcerting.

"Scene of the accident? I was nearly crying yesterday. Why would I smile?"

"Deny all you want, but it's gone viral on the Internet. I'll send the photo to your cell, and you can see for yourself." She snapped her phone off. A few seconds later, a ping was followed by a text message, which he opened. It was a shot of him at the scene of the accident the day before: The Number Three Bridge in ruins, six vehicles, twisted out of shape, rolling in the torrents underneath, one of which was still smoking, while Yang stood by the rubble, grinning broadly. At the bottom of the photo were two lines, the main caption being:

Why are you so pleased when your compatriots have died?

With the sub-caption:

Our Highway Bureau Chief at the scene of an accident.

A buzz tore through Yang's head. Was he really smiling at the scene of the accident, he wondered? He'd been worried sick; how could he have been smiling? Was that really him? It must have been an online prank from someone who had photoshopped an earlier picture of his smiling face onto the accident site. Everyone had been busy saving lives, and he had spent a night at the hospital, so why would anyone pull a prank like that? Yet he could not find any sign of pasting; his image and the backdrop matched seamlessly. It dawned on him that he had been frightened out of his wits when he reached the site and that his mind had gone blank after a tongue-lashing from County Head Du. The mayor had shown up and questioned the quality of the bridge construction, asking for the name of the person responsible for the construction. Du had pointed at Yang and said, "Him," making him freeze in fright, which was why he'd grinned foolishly when the mayor asked him, "Was it you?" Yang had realized how foolish he must have looked at the time and had even felt like kicking himself for the foolish smile. But he'd forgotten all about it when he was at the hospital and saw the number of fatalities climb. How could he have known that someone would take a picture of his foolish grin and post it online? The two captions altered the nature of his smile completely, changing a foolish grin into a pleased smile; he'd been at a loss as to what to say, but now he appeared to be enjoying the scene. Whose damned handiwork was this? This was sneakily substituting one thing for another, a vile case of photo manipulation. Someone had cut and pasted various events, turning them into something else altogether. Yang could not help but shout in the hallway:

"Fuck you!"

A nurse walking out of the ICU was so startled by his outburst she nearly dropped the tray she was holding. Even Yang's deputy, who had stayed close by the whole time, was alarmed. He took the phone from Yang and froze when he saw the picture. He whipped out his own phone and went online. The photo had become headline news on websites nationwide. The grin had instantaneously propelled Yang to the status of the most famous person in the country; moreover, the netizens had already dubbed him "Mr. Smiley Face." Below the photo were thousands of posts that castigated him, said he was devoid of humanity, and called him a beast for not taking a couple of dozen deaths seriously. Would you have looked happy if your father, mother, wife, son and/or daughter had died under the bridge? one asked. They also cursed all eight generations of his ancestors. Yang's position as a bureau chief was even used by some to attack society and government, but the most prevalent comment was:

Fuck you!

The deputy turned to look at Yang, who was slumped in chair, grinning foolishly.

3

Yang found was fond of the saying that blessings never come in pairs, while misfortunes never arrive alone. While he knew that no one enjoys smooth sailing all through life, that there are always twists and turns in anyone's journey, he had never imagined that his twists and turns could have so many hairpin curves. A bureau chief in a county is a minor official, one that had no ranking in Qing-dynasty officialdom, where even a county head was in the seventh and lowest rank. But he had become a celebrity over a foolish grin, even more famous than the provincial party secretary, who was known only in his own province, not beyond. Now everyone in the country knew who Yang Kaituo was; they all knew that Mr. Smiley Face had treated a disaster as a happy event, turned a tragedy into a comedy. Theoretically speaking, the situation was bad enough for Yang, with everything all mixed up—his foolish smile considered a happy expression, and him labeled Mr. Smiley Face. He could not have imagined that this was only the beginning. Someone had zeroed in on his watch, which was visible in the photo, saying it was a famous Swiss brand that cost 150,000 yuan. Then an Internet search turned up photos taken over the past few years of him appearing at county official functions, all focusing on his wrist. No watches were found in recent photos, so they went further back in time to check photos of him at county official functions, producing the result of six different brands of watches, one worth 200,000 yuan, one 300,000 yuan, and one at half a million yuan. There was even one, a top-of-the-line, limited edition that was worth 1.2 million yuan. The total worth of his seven watches was roughly 2.5 million yuan. Following the watch hunt was the revelation of his salary. A cadre at the rank of section chief made 3,100 yuan a month, which gave him a yearly income of under 40,000 yuan. If Yang had bought his seven watches with money earned legally, he would have had to work for six decades, without spending on anything else, food included. His age was revealed. At forty-five, he could not have made enough to afford the watches even if he'd started working right after birth; in fact, he'd have had to start working seventeen or eighteen years in his mother's womb. They gave him another nickname, Mr. Watch-Face. Yang's wristwatches had had nothing to do with the collapse of Number Three Rainbow Bridge, but they were now tightly connected, thanks to the Internet and the mass search. Worse yet, he'd actually stopped wearing a watch since the government's anti-corruption promotion of clean officialdom. He had dug one up to wear on the morning of his nephew's wedding purely to make his sister look good, thinking that it was a private function, not an official occasion. He'd raced to the site when he'd heard about the bridge collapse, too absorbed in the tragedy to remember the watch. He hadn't expected that the Internet and its search would focus on what he forgot. He could not stop himself from cursing:

"Fuck you, Internet."

The pressure of public opinion and Yang's new monikers—Mr. Smiley Face and Mr. Watch-Face—drew the attention of the nation to his city and county. Through mass media, the city announced two decisions: one, an investigative team would be formed to conduct a thorough examination of the bridge collapse and strive to give a responsible answer to the public in the shortest time possible; and two, Yang Kaituo, the highway bureau chief would be under double discipline. A clear explanation of the origin of his seven watches would be given to the public in the shortest time possible.

4

Yang Kaituo was not forewarned that he would be under double discipline since he was working with his staff to clean up the accident site. Known nationwide as Mr. Smiley Face and Mr. Watch-Face, he was an Internet "star." But, convinced that one's shadow is never crooked as long as one stands straight, he decided to ignore the gossip and rumors. As the saying goes, a blameless person has no need to explain oneself, and gossip stops with the wise. He refused to be held hostage by the cruel mobs on the Internet. If ignored, the rumormongers would gradually lose interest and eventually give up, like a dense fog rising from the ground, slowly dissipating as the sun rises. In contrast, any attempt to explain, refute, or fight back would just add fuel to the fire, sending flames shooting high into the air, and one thing would lead to yet another. At the moment, Yang wished there would be a more noteworthy news event, even if it were something terrible, like an earthquake, a mine disaster, or war breaking out between China and Japan over Diaoyu Islands. He would settle for incidents of contaminated milk or a movie star's extramarital affair or whoring around, all of which would overshadow Mr. Smiley Face and Mr. Watch-Face and provide a smoke screen so he could take a breather. But the sky was bright, peace reigned over China, and all the movie stars were behaving themselves. Yang cursed silently:

"Damned bad news. It's nowhere when I need it, and everywhere when I don't."

"Fuck you, bad news!"

Since external forces provided him with no bad news, Yang could only work hard to make up for his missteps or act as if nothing had happened. For two days he traveled along a straight line between two points, dashing from the bridge to the hospital, never making it home to get a good night's sleep. His only consolation was that the medical staff had finally stabilized the condition of the critically injured, and the number of deaths had plateaued. The severity of the incident would not worsen if no more died. He was able to breathe a sigh of relief. At the bridge, he met with engineers and technicians to study the situation and craft a plan for repairs when he wasn't working with the pontoon brigade crew to clean up the site. Over a two-day period, the engineers and technicians had examined the ruined bridge and used jackhammers on cracks in the bridge piers. Yang gave them five days to produce a plan he could take to county and city officials, whose approval, once given, would set the repair work in motion, with an eye to reopening traffic within a month. One morning, Yang's cell phone rang while he was at the accident site. His heart raced when he saw it was County Head Du, who had not stopped screaming at him ever since the accident. He now feared Du even more than he'd feared his mother as a child. An ill-tempered woman, she had yelled and often whipped him. But not taking the call was out of the question, so he picked it up, prepared to be screamed at again. Instead, Du was quite genial:

"Where are you, Old Yang?"

"I'm at the accident site, Sir."

"I hear you have a plan for the repairs. When can I see it?"

Yang was elated to know that Du was aware of what he had been doing. That was a good sign, wasn't it? How wonderful when people work together on something constructive instead of expending energy talking about misleading matters.

"We've been working on the repair plan for two days, but I didn't want to show you yet, since it still doesn't seem thorough enough."

"The provincial and municipal governments want to reopen for traffic as soon as possible. Can you come to the office to talk it over?" Du said.

"I'll be there right away, Sir."

Putting away his phone, Yang picked up the draft repair plan, jumped into his car, and raced to the county seat in high spirits. He went straight to the government building and walked into Du's office, where the county head was joined by two strangers. Assuming they were specialists sent by the provincial or municipal government to inspect the bridge-reopening work, Yang did not pay them much attention. He spread the draft out on the desk, but Du stopped him before he could start explaining:

"Let's put that aside for now, Old Yang." Du pointed to the two men.

"These comrades are from the municipal discipline committee. They want to ask you a couple of things."

Du turned and walked out, leaving a dumbfounded Yang behind. Now he realized he'd fallen for Du's trick of "luring a tiger out of the mountains," using the repair plan as a ruse. Nothing good could come from talking to members of the municipal discipline committee. Looking at Du's departing back, Yang wanted to say something, but did not know what. Du was the only man he knew there, but he had left the office, leaving him with the two strangers from the discipline committee. He could only stammer:

"You want ask me about a couple of things? What are they?"

One of them wore an expressionless face, so did the other, who said:

"Not a couple of things. Just one, actually."

"You are now under double discipline.'"

Again, Yang's head nearly exploded. Double discipline—taken into custody while an investigation was underway. When the discipline committee took you into custody, you were under suspicion, or at least they thought you should be. And you had to wait until after the investigation to know exactly what you were being suspected of. They had said they wanted to ask him a couple of things but had asked him nothing; instead, they were there to inform him of an unalterable outcome. Yang knew that trying to explain or to resist was futile, so he stammered another question:

"Starting when?"

"You'll come with us now."

"But I don't have anything with me. Can I go home to pack a change of clothes and get a toothbrush?"

"No need." The man shook his head. "We have everything ready for you."

"Can I call my wife? I'll tell her I'm away on business," Yang said while taking out his cell phone.

"No need. We'll notify her." More head shaking from the man, who reached out for Yang's phone. Yang hesitated, but knowing he had no choice, he handed over his phone.

They left Du's office, walked downstairs, and climbed into their car. Yang's car was there too; and Yang's driver, exhausted after two hard days, was dozing behind the wheel, oblivious to the fact that his boss was being taken away. After leaving the compound and the county, they headed into the mountains. Where exactly were they going? Yang did not dare ask. The car went up the hills, over the mountain, and into a valley. Seasonal changes arrive later in the mountains, where apricot trees were in full bloom on the hillside. A vista opened before them when they drove out of the valley, and a mirror lake with green ripples came into view. On one side of the lake was a small building, their final destination. Yang knew it was the interrogation site when he saw the door sign for the "Municipal Finance System Training Center." Hostels in remote areas or urban guesthouses were where double-discipline interrogations were conducted. He looked around; not a bad view, at least better than a prison.

They got out of the car. One of the men made a call, and someone came out of the building two minutes later. The newcomer looked Yang over before telling him to come with him. The two men who were responsible for bringing him here got back into the car and roared away. Yang knew that a new group would take over. He followed the man into the building, onto an elevator, and up to the fifth floor, where they got out. They walked to the end of the hallway and stopped at a door. The man knocked and opened the door.

"He's here," he said.

A gaunt, bespectacled middle-aged man behind a desk was looking at a computer screen. Alerted by the announcement, he looked up, glanced at Yang, and nodded for him to enter. Yang walked in and looked around. It was a converted hostel room. The man who had walked him over left. With a cordial look, the bespectacled man pointed at a chair across from his desk.

"Please have a seat, Chief Yang."

Yang felt the tension ease slightly when he heard the man use his title and ask him to sit, for his situation had yet to become a "conflict between opposing forces." After Yang was seated, the man pointed to a video camera in a corner.

"Our conversation will be taped. You don't mind, do you?"

Yang had an instinctual aversion to having his photo taken or being videotaped; after all, the uproar over Mr. Smiley Face and Mr. Watch-Face had both stemmed from a photo taken of him at the scene of an accident getting posted on the Internet. But he knew he could not oppose the use of a video camera during an interrogation. Would they stop taping just because he said no? Would they take it away because he minded? Of course not. The end result would be the same whether he minded or not. So, he shook his head to show he did not.

"Do you know why you're here?" the man asked.

"I do," Yang replied after a brief pause.

"Why?"

"I smiled at a very inappropriate moment two days ago."

The man smiled at his reply.

"What else?"

"And the watches," Yang volunteered when he considered the question and knew he could not pass it off easily.

The man swiveled his computer around so Yang could see the screen, where his seven watches, or the seven watches unearthed by the mass online search, were lined up neatly. The severity of seven crimes arrayed before his eyes was not lost on him.

"Tell me where they all came from," the man said.

Yang had been trying to find a way to explain away the seven watches. Over the past two days, as he shuttled between the bridge and the hospital, studying a repair plan with his bureau staff, he had been hatching an explanation for the watches in case he was asked about them. He had come up with six, but he could not decide which one would offer the most acceptable excuse for having them. Before he could make up his mind, he had come under double discipline, and was too harried to know what to do. Time was not on his side, as the man waited for an answer. Yang had to pick one.

"They belonged to someone else. My maternal grandfather was a watch repairman," he explained, "and I've been fond of watches since childhood. Of course, I couldn't afford any of these watches. I borrowed them from a friend each time and gave it back when I was done.

"Like this watch, the one I wore a few days ago." He pointed to the screen. "My nephew was getting married, and I went to attend the celebration. He's my sister's son and she, my sister, saved my life when I was a kid ..."

He stopped abruptly when he sensed he was digressing. Without a word of criticism, the man simply redirected the conversation:

"Whom did you borrow it from?"

Over the past two days Yang had had great difficulty assigning ownership to each watch. Saying he had borrowed them from friends was easy, but he could not think of anyone who could have owned them. Sure, he'd come up with more than three dozen names, all friends of his, but in the end, he'd crossed them out one by one. Some, like him, would not have enough legal income to afford such a watch. Others could, but their loyalty was not a certainty; he could not be sure that they would help him out, and, during this crisis, might even hit him when he was down. The man waited patiently, so Yang pointed to another watch.

"This one is from a cousin on my mother's side."

"What does he do?"

"He's a wealthy contractor in Africa. He returned a few days ago to attend my nephew's wedding."

"Where is he now?"

"He's gone back to Botswana."

Now that Yang had assigned one of the watches to his cousin in Botswana, the man moved on.

"How about these? Who did you borrow them from?"

Yang could not toss out an answer since he'd yet to come up with suitable owners for the rest, and he knew that a misstep at this moment would open a hole in his story, which would in turn lead to more holes, and eventually blow up his defense, like a collapsing levee.

"The others were from several years ago. I wore them and gave them back. I can't think of their owners off the top of my head."

Instead of pressing him for an answer, the man smiled and said:

"You need time to think of the names, Chief Yang, and you shall have it."

He swiveled the computer back, turned it off, and stood up to put on his jacket. "We'll stop here for today."

Yang got to his feet and asked uncertainly:

"Where do I go now?"

The man picked up the phone on his desk and dialed a number. Two crew-cut young men in jackets walked in; they exuded a no-nonsense air. The middle-aged man pointed at them and said to Yang:

"These are Fang and Yuan. They'll be taking care of you."

"Let's move to a different room, Chief Yang," Fang said.

Yang followed them out. They walked down the hallway and took the elevator to the second floor, where they went to the end of the hallway. Fang opened a door and signaled for Yang to enter. He stepped inside to see that it was standard hostel room, equipped with a bed, a desk, and a chair. On the desk was a pile of documents, to which Yuan pointed and said to Yang:

"Why don't you start with reading those, Chief Yang?"

Yang sat down to read the documents, which turned out to include the party constitution, rules for party members, and his membership application from twenty years before. He had read the first two but was startled to see his application appear out of the blue. After twenty years, he had forgotten all about it and had never expected to see it in a place where he was under double discipline. His curiosity was piqued, as was his admiration for the disciplinary committee's diligence. He laid the first two aside and opened his application. In the upper right-hand corner was a picture of him from back then; he had worn a white shirt and a smile at the corners of his mouth, eyes staring straight ahead. How young he looked! The application was neatly and carefully written in his own handwriting, filled with vows to "work for the welfare of the masses and devote his life to the struggle for Communism." It was clear to him that the organization wanted him to read his own words as a contrast to what he'd been doing in recent years, so he would reflect and repent. Yang wanted to reflect and repent, but weariness stole upon him, after two sleepless days of racing between the accident site and the hospital. He'd been able to stay awake earlier, but he began to feel drowsy at the sight of the bed. He dozed off when he reached the third page of his application, which turned into a blur before his eyes.

"You've got an attitude problem, Chief Yang," Fang said as he poked him awake. "Other comrades under double discipline wail and weep tears of remorse when they read their own applications. How could you doze off?"

Yang woke up and replied abashedly, "I haven't slept in two days."

"We asked you here, Chief Yang, not for you to sleep and rest. We want you to explain yourself and clarify the sources of the seven watches," Yuan said.

"Can I take a little nap first? I'll come clean when I wake up."

"Come clean first, and then you can sleep."

"My head is filled with mush. How can I recall something from back then?"

Yuan looked over at Fang, who asked Yang:

"Are you man of your word?"

"I am. If not, you can stand me against the wall and never let me sleep again," Yang promised.

"Very well then, Chief Yang. We'll let you sleep. We believe in your political awareness."

Yang left the desk and fell onto the bed. Fang picked up the documents and walked out, while Yuan pulled a chair to sit facing the bed. Yang knew Fang stayed to watch him sleep in case he tried to kill himself.

"Go get some rest, Yuan. I won't do anything stupid," Yang said.

"I have to follow the rules."

"I'm sorry to put you through the trouble."

Yang turned and fell asleep. A long time later he was startled awake. The room's lights were on, and Fang had taken Yuan's place.

"You're awake, Chief Yang."

Still groggy from the sleep, Yang nodded.

"You can now explain the sources of the watches."

The cobwebs in Yang's head whisked away. He was in a jam again, for he still could not think of anyone he could trust. The awkward silence went on for five minutes, until Fang said:

"Obviously Chief Yang is *not* a man of his word." He pointed to the wall across from the bed. "We'll follow your promise then. No more sleep for you. Stand up so you can clear your head."

Yang got up from the bed and walked over to stand against the wall, which felt soft. After feeling around with his hand, he discovered that it was cushioned with soft material. That he knew was to prevent those under double discipline from taking the easy way out. Two hours went by, and Yuan came in to replace Fang. He sat down and stared at Yang for two hours; when the effects of standing got to Yang, he quietly lowered himself to a squatting position to ease the discomfort. Yuan was reading his cell phone. He looked up the moment Yang was on his haunches.

"Have you recalled the sources of the watches now, Chief Yang?"

Yang scrambled to his feet and stood back up against the wall. A long time passed as the sky began to lighten up outside. He suddenly felt hungry, realizing he hadn't eaten since leaving the bridge a day and a night ago. Fang and Yuan must have forgotten to offer him food. Hunger did not bother him when he wasn't thinking about food, but once the thought occurred him, his stomach felt as if it were collapsing in on itself. Feeling weak all over, he said to Yuan:

"Could I have something to eat? I haven't had a bite to eat since yesterday."

"You can eat when you recall where the watches came from."

Yang continued to stand against the wall with an empty stomach, something he had experienced as a child, but not over the past four decades. Now the feeling had returned: a horde of insects crawling, biting, and shouting angrily in his stomach. Yang sighed and tried to ignore the pangs. Hunger induced fatigue, which in turn sent him back down to the floor and earned a knock on the desk from Yuan. He snapped awake and quickly straightened up. More time passed. Finally unable to hold on any longer, he oozed down to the floor like mud. And that was where he stayed. The door opened, and Fang came in. Yang said to him:

"Can I have something to eat first? I'll tell you everything about the watches once I eat."

"No!" Yuan banged on the desk. "You lied to us about the nap."

"I won't lie again."

"Tell us first, or no food. And don't get any ideas," Yuan said.

"I'm dizzy from hunger. How can I recall anything?"

"Everybody makes mistakes, and everybody is allowed to correct them," Fang cut in. "Let's give Chief Yang one more chance."

Yuan left the room and returned ten minutes later with a large platter of rice and a big bowl of steaming braised pork.

"You have to keep your promise this time, Chief Yang," Fang said.

Yang's stomach came back alive at the sight of food, and so did the insects inside. With a nod, he finished off the rice and pork in no time. Yuan retrieved the empty bowl and platter.

"Shall we start, Chief Yang?" Fang said.

Yang looked down wordlessly, not because he did not want to tell them, but because he still had no one to whom he could assign ownership. Fang heaved a sigh, so did Yuan, as Yang went back to stand against the wall. An hour later, a powerful thirst assailed him from the salty pork he had consumed. He needed water, as he wondered if the kitchen had added salt on purpose. After going back on his word twice, he could not bring himself to ask for water. Fang left the room, leaving Yuan to guard him. Yuan drank from a water bottle as he read his cell phone. Yang could bear prolonged thirst but only when no one around him was drinking; seeing Yuan doing just that aggravated every cell in his body. He had felt terrible before the meal, but now thirst was ten times worse. Insects were not only gnawing at every nerve and cell, but they were also sucking away every last bit of moisture in him. Finally, he could stand it no longer.

"Can I have some water. I'll come clean once I have some."

"We've been tricked twice already." Yuan sneered. "Never again."

That shut Yang up effectively. It grew dark outside little by little. An hour later, Yang was like a towel with the last drop of water wrung out; his head felt scorched, while his body had turned into a bundle of dry kindling that threatened to burst into flames. He gasped for air, mouth open, and a sudden dizziness made him slump to the floor. He struggled to stand when Yuan banged on the desk. The door opened to let in two people. Thirst was sending sparks to his head, but he could tell that Fang was not among them. He did not know who they were, but a closer look told him that one was a man and the other a woman. The man stood by the door while the woman froze at the sight of Yang. It took her a full two minutes to recover, after which she raced over and shouted:

"Kaituo!"

The voice told Yang the woman running at him was his sister. She ran too fast, and they fell to the floor together. When she got up, she put her arms around him and said, "What has happened to you, Kaituo?"

Yang was so thirsty he felt as if his body was smoking, a sensation that transported him back to the time when he was a year old: after contracting meningitis, he was at death's door, so his mother left him in a grass hut to his own fate. His sister, who was nine at the time, came to the hut, cradled him, and gave him water to drink. In her arms again, he had a feeling that they were back in the old days.

"I'm thirsty, Sis," he stammered.

But, unlike the earlier time, his sister did not have water to give him now. She turned to look at the man at the door, and Yang saw it was the bespectacled man who had interrogated him. He signaled to Yuan, who picked up a bottle of water from the desk and handed it to Yang's sister. She twisted the cap off and held it up for Yang to drink. Taking big, noisy gulps, he drained the bottle. Infused with the water, the cells in his body seemed to revive and his nerves were revitalized. He caught his breath. "That feels so good, Sis."

She began to cry. "Tell them everything, Kaituo. It's better than staying in this room. Even if you go to prison, at least you'd have water and you can see the sun. I'll come visit you every month."

5

Before the interrogation recommenced, the bespectacled man let Yang drink his fill, after which he was allowed a shower and given a change of clothes, all provided by the organization. Then the kitchen prepared a bowl of noodles sprinkled with chopped emerald-green onions and cilantro. Picking up some noodles with his chopsticks, he saw an egg nestled underneath. This time the food was seasoned just right, not too salty; it even had a splash of vinegar. When Yang sat back down before the man, he was a new man from top to bottom, and his stomach no longer cried out for food or water.

Once again, the man turned the computer screen so that Yang could see the seven watches, still lined up neatly.

"Who gave you these watches?"

Yang rattled off seven names.

"What for?"

"I gave them construction work."

"What was it?"

Yang described several projects.

"What else did they give you?"

"Nothing else." Yang shook his head.

The man frowned. "I see Chief Yang needs a couple more days to think it over." He stood up and put on his jacket, scaring Yang, who jumped to his feet and stopped him.

"Now I remember."

Taking off his jacket before sitting down, the man continued:

"What else?"

"Gold, jewelry, fine clothing and bags, gift certificates," Yang answered after sitting down.

His eyes fixed on Yang, the man nodded and persisted:

"What else?"

Yang glanced at the man and replied after a brief pause, "And cash."

"Who gave you money and how much?"

"I'll have to try to recall each."

The man picked up his teacup and took a sip. "Take your time."

Five minutes later, Yang said hesitatingly:

"It's been such a long time I can't recall everything precisely. It'd be a wrongful accusation if I didn't get it right."

"Not to worry. We'll verify every item."

Yang gave him names and amounts before ending with, "I've told you everything. You can beat me to death, but I won't have more to offer."

"I believe you, Chief Yang." The man smiled. "Have some tea."

Yang picked up his cup and took a drink.

"I have one more little question," the man said.

"What is it?"

The man opened his drawer and took out a cell phone. One look told Yang it was his phone, which the men from the disciplinary committee had confiscated in County Head Du's office. The man brought up a text message and showed Yang, who saw it had been sent ten days before by someone named Su Shuang.

Elder Brother → Pure gold → Hurry over

Yang froze.

"The area code is the provincial capital, but what does it mean?"

Yang hung his head wordlessly.

"Who is Su Shuang?"

Yang remained silent, still looking down.

"I was hoping we could get everything straightened out today, but obviously you need more time," the man said as he stood up again and started to put on his jacket. Yang stopped him.

"I'll tell you, Sir."

The man took off his jacket and sat down. "Go ahead."

"I—it's awkward." Yang hesitated.

"We're alone. Go ahead, tell me."

"Please don't misunderstand, but the pure gold in the message isn't money, it's a golden girl. It means she'd found a woman for me in the city."

"Are you saying Su Shuang is a pimp?"

"You can say that," Yang said after thinking it over.

The man slammed his hand on the desk and said with a stern look:

"The provincial city is over four hundred kilometers from your county, and half of it in the mountains, so it takes a whole day to get there. You'd drive a whole day for a call girl? Who's going to believe that? You have call girls in your county, don't you?"

Yang was nearly choking. "Yes, we do," he admitted tearfully, "but Su Shuang's girls are different."

"How are they different? Are they prettier?"

"Yes, and something else too," Yang said haltingly.

"What else?"

"They're not call girls. They're virgins."

The man was appalled. He banged the desk again.

"You're corrupt to the core, Yang Kaituo. You don't just want call girls when you go whoring. You have to have virgins."

"That's not it," Yang said with his head down.

"What is it then?"

"I'm embarrassed to tell you."

"Tell me," the man roared.

"I've been frail since I was young. and I'm no good in the you-know-what. But I get energized, like getting an infusion of chicken blood when it comes to virgins. I could stay vigorous for a month after having sex with a virgin."

The man looked dumbfounded before saying, "So it's a cure for you?"

"You could say that," Yang stammered. "So, you see, there's a reason."

The man laughed, despite his anger, but quickly wiped off the smile. "It's not going to be that simple, Chief Yang. Su Shuang found you virgins, and you should be paying her. But we checked your bank account, and found, instead, that she has wired you money ten times over the past six years. Why is that?"

Yang lowered his head again and said nothing for a moment before stammering a reply, "I gave her construction projects."

"What projects?"

"Actually, she didn't want the projects for herself. She was just a go-between who handed the jobs off to a certain construction company in the provincial city."

"What did you give her?"

Yang told him.

"Did they get the Number Three Rainbow Bridge job?"

"Yes, but they turned around and contracted it out," Yang said softly.

The man nodded while taking back Yang's cell phone and turned off the computer. "We'll stop here, Chief Yang." He stood up to put on his jacket. Yang remained seated this time as he asked, "I don't understand, Sir."

Surprised, the man took off his jacket and sat back down, "What do you mean?"

"I deleted the text ten days ago. How come it's back on my cell?"

"What do you think?" The man asked with a smile.

Now Yang understood that if they could obtain his banking information, they could call up every message in his cell phone. "I have another question, Sir."

"What is it?"

"I want to know who posted the picture of me with my foolish smile."

"Someone in the crowd, of course. There were so many people looking on at the site of the accident. And everyone has a cell phone these days."

"I've been thinking about that for days, and I'm convinced it wasn't one of the onlookers," Yang said with a shake of his head.

"Then who?"

"Someone who wanted me to be the scapegoat for the fatalities," Yang fumed. "I didn't even know when they accused me of taking bribes," he shouted. "They're the fucking corrupt ones."

"You can report them to the disciplinary committee if you have evidence."

"I'll be going to prison soon, so how am I supposed to collect evidence," Yang said tearfully. "They knew that. They're evil." He continued, "Besides, I have to think about my wife and son when I'm in prison."

The man got up again and put on his jacket. "We seem to be getting sidetracked, Chief Yang. Don't you think?"

Yang did not respond.

Chapter 5

Niu Xiaoli

1

Niu Xiaoli opened an eatery in town called "Xiaoli's Diner." Everyone knew that, despite weeks of hardship during her search, she had finally located Song Caixia. By carrying out a sham marriage, Song had made it possible for Niu to file a lawsuit in the local court against her. Eventually, Song was ordered to pay back the 100,000 yuan, plus another 20,000 yuan for emotional damage, expenses Niu had incurred for traveling from her hometown to Qinhan County, and her wages from missing work. Song's family did not have the cash, so the court stepped in and sold their house, enabling Niu Xiaoli to come home with 120,000 yuan. Her feat was widely talked about in town. In addition to paying off the debt she owed Tu Xiaorui, the illegal loan shark, she had enough money left over to set up a diner, which opened for business on July 8th. Ten days later, she and Feng Jinhua were married, a virtual double-happiness. Her only problem was Old Xin, from Xin Family Village, who had been pestering her ever since she returned. Before she opened the diner in town, he went to Niu Family Village to see her every day, though he never caused a scene, except to say:

"Give me back my wife and my son."

His wife was, of course, Zhu Juhua, who had gone with Xiaoli to look for Song Caixia, and his son was Little Monkey, the four-year-old who had tagged along. The first time Xin came to see her about his family, Xiaoli fumed:

"You want your wife and son back? Well, so do I. She stole the travel money I'd sewn in her underwear. Pay me the 3,000 yuan before we talk about giving back your wife and son."

"I'm going to sue you." Xin stomped his foot.

"Go ahead. Your marriage is illegal. Your wife was bought for you, and you kept her around. That amounts to unlawful captivity. I'm sure the public security bureau would like to know about that."

He went quiet for a while before speaking up:

"How's this? I'll do what you did when you were looking for Song Caixia. I'll pay for the travel expenses, and you travel with me to bring them back."

"You're a grown man. You can get on the road yourself. Why do you need her to take you there?" Niu Xiaoli's fiancé said.

"She went looking for Song and found her. She has experience."

"We're about to open a diner in town. We're busy," Feng said.

"Each day my wife and son are away, I'll spend it squatting outside your door." Emphasizing his stubborn streak, Xin sat on his haunches at Niu's door and continued, "You lost them, so you have to get them back for me."

"You were missing only one person. I have two," he added.

After Xiaoli opened for business, Xin squatted daily by the diner door. Before her return, Xiaoli had anticipated that he would pester her about his wife and son. But she had not expected him to follow her from the village into town, as punctually as going to work.

"You can squat by her door back in Niu Family Village any time you want," Feng told him. "But we're running a diner here. Do you know how it affects our business to have you sitting there like a dog?"

"I don't have to squat here or anywhere." Xin said, looking up at the new diner entrance. "I spent 70,000 yuan on a wife three years ago. Give me the money and I'll be gone."

"She conned you, why should we pay you?" Niu felt like laughing in spite of her annoyance at Xin.

"Watch yourself, or I'll pick you up by the scruff of your neck and toss you into the river," Feng said after giving him two kicks. "Again."

Xin stood up after a look at Feng, walked off, and squatted in an empty lot across the street. Niu and Feng had to laugh.

"Squat there for a whole year and you'll earn my respect," Feng said.

Xiaoli's Diner was located in front of the entrance to the garment factory where she'd once worked. The factory's four hundred employees worked in two shifts, keeping the machinery running nonstop. Back when she'd been one of them, she'd taken lunch or dinner by rushing to a stand at the entrance to buy a flatbread or a meat-stuffed bun. Both were delicious, but too dry, causing a constant thirst for water after she went back to work. When she'd gone searching for Song Caixia, she'd spent two fruitless weeks there before leaving for another provincial city with Su Shuang, where she'd stayed for about three weeks. While there, she'd frequented riverside diners with Su and other girls, where she'd discovered a local dish called "sheep offal soup." It tasted wonderful, especially when eaten with fried flatbreads. She'd looked into how it was made.

Upon returning home, she did two things: one, she stopped working at the garment factory, and two, she rented a two-room house by the factory entrance to open a diner specializing in sheep offal soup and fried flatbreads. She referred to the money she had brought back with her as compensation from Song Caixia and told people that 108,800 yuan of the sum went to pay Tu Xiaorui back. But, in fact, she only gave Tu 99,200 yuan. Tu had lent her the money at the monthly rate of 3 percent, which had been reduced to 2 percent when he'd stuck his tongue into her mouth on the day she borrowed it. Feng and Xiaoli's brother, Niu Xiaoshi, knew that the capital for the diner was 16,000 yuan, though she actually had 25,600 yuan. A bowl of soup cost two yuan, the flatbreads 50 fen each, which brought in 50 fen more than a flatbread or a stuffed bun alone. Only a handcart was needed to sell flatbreads or stuffed buns for standing customers. Xiaoli's Diner was a real eatery, with tables and chairs for customers to sit and eat. She supplied free soup refills, so everyone got enough hot soup to finish the meal, after which their faces were covered with sweat. Factory women started showing up to eat soon after she opened, and she gave up on serving flatbreads and stuffed buns alone. She also drew customers from the bathhouse to the right of the factory entrance. Customers who felt hungry either before or after a bath would opt for the fare at her diner. There were also the bathhouse employees, including back-scrubbers, the pedicurists, even women from up north who provided "special services." After getting to know the bathhouse owner better, Xiaoli began delivering food to his place. As business grew, she slowly forgot about Xin squatting in the nearby lot until, after two months, she noticed that he had been showing up less frequently. Instead of coming daily, he now only made an afternoon presence once in a while. She asked around and learned that he had not given up on pestering her but rather had simply realized that time was money. He had no income if he didn't carry bricks. So, he went back to the Xin Family Village kiln, coming to the empty lot only occasionally to show he had not forgotten about his family. On this afternoon, when she came out of the diner to use the toilet, she saw him squatting there again, so she walked up and noticed the crude protective headgear from the kiln on his head. It was the height of summer, but he was still wearing his work outfit—padded jacket and cotton shoes.

"It's the middle of summer, Old Xin. Aren't you hot wearing that?"

He ignored her, rolling his eyes. But when she returned from the toilet, she saw he had taken off his helmet and that his face was streaked with dust. The skin on his arms was splotchy and pale.

Summer was replaced by fall, and three months went by, when she realized that she hadn't seen Xin for more than a month. She gradually put him out of her mind, thinking that he'd had a change of heart after months of fruitless squatting. One night, when she came out of the shop to use the toilet, she saw a dark object curled up on the empty lot. She thought it had to be a stray dog waiting for leftovers tossed from her diner, but when she walked by and took a closer look, it turned out to be a man sleeping on the ground. It was Xin. A gust of wind blew over, raised a column of dust, and settled back down on his face. In fact, there was dust in his eyes and nostrils. She bent over to rouse him, giving him a fright when he opened his eyes and saw her.

"Have you eaten, Old Xin?"

He rubbed his eyes and shook his head.

She walked back inside to grab a flatbread, filled a bowl with soup, and carried them out to him. After a glance at her, he took them and started eating.

"You haven't been here in a long time. How come?"

He put down the soup and began to wail, to her surprise.

"I went to that other province," he said tearfully.

That came as a shock.

"Did you find Zhu Juhua and Little Monkey?"

"The address she gave me is fake," he replied with a shake of his head, before adding, "I didn't want to give up, so I spent two weeks searching all over Qinhan County. There are twelve towns and townships there, with about a hundred women named Zhu Juhua, but none of them was my wife."

The same experience Niu had had six months earlier.

"You'll just have try again someday," she offered.

"I came here to wait till you close up because I want to ask you something," he said with a tilt of his head.

"What?"

"How did you find Song Caixia? When I couldn't find my wife in Qinhan, I went to Song's village, only to learn that she also gave a fake address."

Not knowing how to respond, she was quiet before finally saying:

"The fake address cost me over a month looking in vain. I found her purely by accident."

"I tried to call you from Qinhan, but I couldn't get through. How come?"

She had gotten a new number after her return but did not feel like giving it to someone like him.

"We're so busy here at the diner I have no time to check my phone."

"I don't want to give up. Can you give me Song's real address? She knew my wife, so I want to make another trip. If I can find Song, I'll find my wife and Little Monkey."

"I demanded compensation from Song's family when I was in Qinhan, so the government auctioned off their house. Who knows where they've gone now that they have no place in live," she replied.

"So that's it, my last lead." He smacked the ground and continued with a sigh. "What do I do now?"

"Are you coming back here tomorrow?" she asked.

"I spent everything on the trip, so I have to go back to carrying bricks."

"How about coming to work at my diner?"

He had a surprised look.

"If you work at my diner, you can keep an eye on me, so no need to make a special trip to squat here. And you're safe from the elements when doing the dishes and cleaning vegetables, better than carrying bricks."

He had a dubious look. "You're not trying to trick me, are you?"

Xiaoli chuckled. "You're penniless, as you said. What do you think I can get out of you? I feel sorry seeing you at the end of your tether.

"It's up to you," she added.

2

Xiaoli had gone through several helpers since opening her diner, starting with her own brother, Xiaoshi. Knowing the job would bring in good money, he was happy to take it, but gave it up before two months had passed. The brother and sister worked side by side; she was in charge of making the food and handling the money, while he served and bused the tables. He liked his job because it did not require much thought or hard work, and he voluntarily picked stems off the vegetables and swept the floor when business was slack. When his sister baked flatbreads, he added firewood when needed and sprinkled chopped coriander on top of the bowls of soup she scooped out. What he found insufferable was the teasing from the diners. He'd been helpless after his wife ran off and had had to rely on his sister's effort to make up for the damage. Worse yet, he'd lost not one, but two wives. His first wife, with whom he'd gone to the city for work, had run off with another man, leaving their young child for him to care for. The desertion of two women added a hint of mystique to his life, while his sister gained legendary status after her long-distance trek to get his wife back. The two storied lives drew customers to the diner for the soup but also to get a good look at the proprietors, though for different reasons. They wanted to see what the capable woman was like and what a wimp her brother was. There are limits to what one can gain from looking at a competent woman, but a great deal with a wimpy man. So, more customers came to check him out than to take a look at her, which he did not notice at first. When a diner came in and placed his order, Xiaoshi brought out the food before going back to help his sister in the kitchen. The diner would shout:

"I need some vinegar." Or,

"How about some hot peppers?"

He'd emerge with a bottle of vinegar or the peppers, giving the diners another opportunity to scrutinize him. After too many such occurrences, he started seeing something else in their eyes. Annoyed, he asked his sister to buy a dozen bottles of vinegar, enough for each table. Then he had her fry more peppers, so he could put a bowl on each table, depriving the diners of the excuse to ask for more of either. But the eatery promised unlimited, free soup refills, which gave the customers a pretext for bringing Xiaoshi out of the kitchen so they could take another look at him. He knew something was up when he saw that customers were not finishing their refilled bowls.

"You asked for refills, but you don't finish them," he complained, banging the bowls when he cleared the tables. "You're treating me like a trained monkey, aren't you?"

The novelty wore off after a month, when the customers lost interest in him and only asked for refills as needed. But it had sown the seeds of suspicion, and he continued to believe they were toying with him whenever he was asked to add more soup. One day, the deliveryman Jiao came for lunch after running around town delivering packages. Parched from the hard work, he had four refills, an innocent act that Xiaoshi took as a ploy to tease him. He grumbled when he noticed that Jiao's fourth bowl was only half finished.

"A hungry ghost in his previous life, and a freeloader now."

Jiao, who was about to walk out the door, erupted when he heard Xiaoshi. He turned and pointed at the note over the door:

Free Unlimited Soup Refills

"Is that a lie?" He added, "Why should I take insults over a few drops of stinky soup?"

Indignation that had accumulated over days sent Xiaoshi into a rage. He pointed at Jiao and fumed:

"Watch your mouth. I'll give you a good licking if you don't shut up. Don't think I won't."

"You must have picked up some skills since I last saw you. Do you even know what it means to give someone a good licking?"

Jiao picked up a vinegar bottle and flung it at Xiaoshi's head. It missed and smashed on the floor, spilling its contents. The other diners rushed over to break up the fight, as did Xiaoli, who had been baking flatbreads. After more verbal combat, Jiao spat on the floor and pointed at Xiaoshi:

"We're not done yet. I'll be back to take care of you, wimp."

He stormed out while Xiaoshi snatched the sign about free unlimited refills off the wall, tore it in half, and squatted down.

"I've had enough of this chicken-shit business. I quit."

The smell of something burning spread into the room, obviously from the flatbreads Xiaoli had left baking on the stove. Seeing that her brother was not cut for her line of business, Xiaoli sent him back to Niu Village and bought him a flock of sheep to tend along the floodplain. Spending all day with sheep and staying away from people kept him out of trouble. After her brother left, Xiaoli thought she could get her fiancé, her soon-to-be husband, to work alongside her, turning the shop into a husband-and-wife business. But Feng did not want to give up his motor scooter repair business, not because he'd have to abandon the shop but because he did not want to give up his mechanic skills.

"As the saying goes, a simple skill is better than a thousand acres of good land," he said. "And there's another saying about not putting all your eggs in one basket. You run your diner while I repair motor scooters, and we'll be covered if something goes wrong at one place."

She had to agree that he made sense, but business was growing too much for one person to handle. For a while she considered hiring a former coworker from the garment factory, but she changed her mind, worrying that the new dynamics of friends turning into boss and employee would be hard to deal with. The closer the friends, the more likely working together would give rise to jealousy. Her friend might not be jealous when the eatery wasn't doing well, but she would likely begrudge her success in business when things were good. She wanted to avoid that kind of potential trouble, which existed not only among former coworkers but also among relatives and neighbors back home. Her plan to find a helper was wrought with so many concerns. In the end, she put up a help-wanted ad outside the diner, which drew a dozen applicants the following morning—some women, some men. She did not like any of them. One looked useless, one slovenly, one difficult, and one lazy. A woman in her early thirties showed up in the afternoon. With a pleasant face, she was neat and clean and looked like she would be fast on her feet; she was well-spoken with a gentle demeanor. As she asked the woman where she came from, Xiaoli hid how positive she was feeling about her.

"You don't recognize me?"

Xiaoli looked at her and shook her head.

"My name is Qi Yafen. I used to sell flatbreads by the factory entrance. You were one of my customers back when you worked there."

A closer look jogged Xiaoli's memory.

"Why did you stop selling flatbreads?"

"No one wanted to buy them after you opened up shop," Qi said.

Xiaoli had ruined the woman's business. Worried that Qi might bear a grudge, Xiaoli decided not to hire her. As if she could read Xiaoli's mind, Yafen said:

"I'm glad I'm not doing that anymore. Now I don't have to set up the stand every day or worry about the elements. I had to pick up and leave every time the weather changed." She added, "I prefer working for someone, because running a business is risky. It's secure working for someone whether there's a flood or drought."

That made sense to Xiaoli.

"Feng Jinhua's older sister and I were middle school classmates. You can ask them about me if you're worried," Qi said, before adding, "I wanted to take a break after all these years of hard work, but I'm a single mother after my divorce three years ago. I spent all my savings renovating my house last month."

Xiaoli thought her story was plausible, so she leaned toward hiring her.

"How much would you want a month?"

"Two thousand yuan. How does that sound?"

Two thousand yuan a month was two hundred more than a worker earns at the garment factory, but it was not an unreasonable amount because there was more to do at the diner. When Xiaoli asked Feng about Yafen that night, he said:

"It's your shop, so you're in charge. But if it were me, I wouldn't hire someone I got to know this way."

But that was how she'd gotten to know everyone in town. So, she called Yafen and offered her the job. Yafen came to work the following morning, and Xiaoli immediately felt a load taken off her shoulders. Baking bread was not all that different from frying it, which Yafen knew well, so she learned to bake bread in three days. Xiaoshi had been too clumsy for such meticulous work, which was why Xiaoli had him serving and busing the tables. Now with Yafen making and baking the bread, Xiaoli could focus on cooking the soup and still have time to serve and bus the tables, a job that did not require any thought. Yafen was a fast learner. After mastering the skill of baking bread, she learned from Xiaoli how to cook the soup and could produce something decent in two weeks. A month later, she took over the kitchen, making both the bread and the soup, and relieving Xiaoli to take care of the customers. As the business grew, Xiaoli hired an older man, Old Sun, to bus the tables and do the dishes, while she greeted the customers and handled the money matters. Sitting behind the counter to watch her employees busy themselves with a throng of noisy diners, she finally felt like a real business owner. But three months later, she discovered that Sun had sticky fingers; he was given to stealing frozen soup or leftover bread. So, she fired him. That was when she noticed Xin sleeping on the empty lot. Feeling sorry for an honest man who was at the end of his tether and somewhat responsible for letting Zhu Juhua and Little Monkey run off, she offered him a job with the same salary she'd paid Sun, 1,500 yuan a month. She watched him carefully on his first day at work and saw that, despite his short stature, he was quick with his hands and feet, carrying the plates and bowls and washing them afterward. And he was a hard worker. When business was slow, he picked up a broom to sweep the floor inside and the ground outside all the way to the empty lot where he'd once squatted. He was a much better worker than the thieving Sun.

"Tired, Old Xin?" Xiaoli asked him at the end of the day.

He wiped the sweat off his forehead, not saying a word.

"It can't be any more tiring than carrying bricks at the kiln," Yafen said.

"I don't mind being tired," Xin said. "The difference is, the bricks were so hot I got blistered all over, but my skin is fine here."

That drew smiles. Xin Village was fifteen li away, which meant he had to ride his bike over early in the morning and back after the eatery closed late at night. It was too tiring, so three days later Xiaoli told him to bring his bedroll and sleep in the shop, an arrangement that would save him the travel and provide someone to keep watch over the diner. Xin was happy to comply, for he lived alone, with his wife and son gone. There was no bed in the shop, but he could simply push two tables together and spread out his bedding for a good night's sleep. Soon two weeks passed. One afternoon between meals, when there were no customers, Xiaoli and Yafen were inside picking the vegetables while Xin was sweeping the ground outside. Yafen whispered to Xiaoli that Xin had not been sleeping in the shop.

"Where has he been sleeping?" Xiaoli asked after recovering from the surprising news.

Yafen pointed to the bathhouse across the way.

"How did you find that out?"

"I didn't see anyone in the shop when I came to start the fire this morning. I thought he'd gone to the toilet, so imagine my surprise when I saw him sneak in from the bathhouse. He was embarrassed when he saw me."

Xiaoli knew there were girls from up north at the bathhouse, so Xin must have gotten himself hooked up with one of them. When she ran into the owner outside her diner that afternoon, Xiaoli made a discreet inquiry and learned that Xin was not at the bathhouse because of a girl. Instead, he had got another job: when the water was let out of the bathing pool at night after all the bathers were gone, Xin would come to scrub the pools with a soft brush and then the toilets with a wire brush. It took two hours to clean each pool and toilet, which meant four hours total to scrub both men's and women's sides. At five yuan per hour, he earned twenty yuan a night. Xiaoli realized that Xin had a good head on his shoulders. It took him barely two weeks to learn everything about the people and the surrounding area and even get himself another job. At the same time, she was worried he might not do as good a job at her shop when he had his feet on two boats, working day and night. When they closed up that night, she told Yafen to leave while she stayed to clean up the kitchen. As she put the leftover soup and vegetables in the refrigerator, she said to Xin in a light tone:

"I hear you haven't been sleeping in here, Old Xin."

His face turned red as he stammered a response:

"I scrub the pools at the bathhouse."

His directness impressed her, so she said:

"Are you getting enough sleep, working day and night?"

"I haven't needed much sleep ever since I was a kid." He added, "I've been working there for a week now, but have you ever seen me doze off?"

Xiaoli had to admit that she hadn't, nor had it affected his job.

"You're working day and night, so you can go look for your wife and son?"

She was surprised to see him shake his head.

"No? You're not looking for them anymore?"

"I want to, but I know I won't find them. It's a waste of money." He sighed before adding, "It took me a while after I got back, but I finally realized that she ran away because she didn't want to stay. It can't be easy trying to find someone who hides from you."

"That's the way to look at it. No need to get hung up on a woman." She added, "Why work so hard when you're not looking for them anymore? Stop going to scrub the bathhouse pools."

"I have to work so hard because I'm not looking for them."

"What do you mean?"

"Buying Juhua cost me 70,000 yuan, which I borrowed from friends and relatives. I've paid back 30,000 yuan, which leaves more than half unpaid. Then I spent over 3,000 yuan on my search for them, so now I'm about 40,000 yuan in debt. That's a lot of money." He continued, "I thought when I found her, I could get her to pay me back if she didn't want to come home with me. But now I have no wife and no money, and I still have to pay off the debt."

Xiaoli had been in a similar predicament when she left with Su Shuang for another provincial capital after failing to find Song Caixia.

"You're not a very nice person," Xin said.

"What do you mean?" Xiaoli asked.

"You won't tell me how you found Song Caixia." He continued, "You found her and made her give you so much money, while I have nothing, like having the hen fly off after the eggs are broken."

Naturally, Xiaoli could not tell him the truth because, like him, she had failed in her search. All she could say was:

"I can't tell you because I just bumped into her. How can I teach you to do that?"

Xin fell silent for a while and heaved a sigh.

"I don't think I'll ever see her and Little Monkey again. I don't mind not seeing her, but I do miss the boy."

Xiaoli knew Little Monkey was not Xin's biological son, that Zhu had brought him along when she married Xin. She also recalled what Zhu had said about Xin's performance in bed.

"He's not your son, so why do you miss him?"

"You're right, he's not, but I grew fond of him after all the time we spent together." He continued, "When he was around, he poked his head out from under the blanket and told me everything until he fell asleep."

He turned to stare into the darkness outside.

"I wonder if he's fallen asleep now."

Xiaoli went home, while Xin cleaned up the shop and then went to scrub pools. After their talk, he no longer hid his night job from her and even sounded unapologetic when he mentioned it. She had to laugh despite her displeasure.

Time passed quickly; soon it was summer again, and people began to come out after nightfall. Xiaoli had light bulbs strung up outside the diner and laid out tables and stools all the way to the empty lot where Xin had once squatted. Her nighttime diner opened for business and sold as many as three hundred bowls of soup a day. The business grew by 30 percent, with the addition of beer and cold dishes. Yafen seemed unfocused, she discovered, and even ruined a pot of soup one evening. Xiaoli was not upset when she asked:

"What's the matter, Yafen?"

"There is something, but I didn't want to bring it up."

"What is it?"

"We're so busy here I shouldn't mention it, but my aunt is sick in the hospital. I'd like to go see her. My mother died when I was young, and my aunt raised me."

"Don't feel bad about mentioning something like that. Go see her tomorrow morning."

Yafen cheered up.

"You can see how busy we are here, so come back as soon as you can."

But three days passed, and there was no sight of her. When Xiaoli called her, Yafen hemmed and hawed until she finally told Xiaoli she did not want to come back. Xiaoli was surprised and felt that there was something fishy about Yafen's sick aunt.

"What have you heard?"

"Nothing."

"Have I done something to make you unhappy?"

"No. Everything's fine."

"Do you want a raise?"

"No, it has nothing to do with any of that. I just don't want to come back."

There was nothing Xiaoli could do about Yafen's decision. With her gone, she had to hire another helper, a woman in her forties named Luo Darong. Luo was a good worker, though not as nimble as Yafen, which required more attention on Xiaoli's part. All in all, however, the day and night business were not affected much. Still in the dark about Yafen's reason to quit, Xiaoli gradually forgot about her, until a month later, another diner opened at the rear entrance of the garment factory. Called Yafen's Eatery, it sold sheep offal soup and baked flatbreads and had a sign on the wall that said "Unlimited Free Soup Refills." Qi Yafen also had tables set up outside at night. Xiaoli's diners decreased by a third. She nearly fainted when she realized the real reason behind Yafen's departure, as well her decision to come work for her. Yafen looked pleasant on the outside, but she had the heart of a snake or a scorpion. You can never tell a person by her looks, Xiaoli said unhappily to her husband, whose older sister had been Yafen's schoolmate.

"Go take a look at the rear entrance of the factory. You can see what your sister's schoolmate did."

"You really can't tell a person by their looks," Feng tsk-tsked. "I told you not to hire her when she came for the interview, but you wouldn't listen. She sold fried flatbreads for three or four years until you came along and drove her out. Now she's opened a diner—an eye for an eye."

Xiaoli had to agree. Qi had bided her time for revenge by working for her for over six months. She had every right to open a diner and sell the same thing; it was not against the law. Xiaoli could only sigh. On the following afternoon before dinner, when there were no customers and Luo Darong had gone into town to buy plasters for her achy shoulder, Xin came to see her.

"I want to tell you something, but promise you won't lose your temper."

"What is it?"

"I think something's going between your husband and Qi Yafen."

Again she nearly fainted.

"What do you mean?"

"They're an item now," Xin said.

"Watch your mouth, Old Xin. I'm not sure about Qi Yafen, but I know my husband. We're together all the time."

"As they say, you can never tell a person by his looks."

"This is serious. You need proof."

"I've seen it with my own eyes."

Maybe she should take him seriously.

"Where?"

"Here, in the shop."

Xiaoli nearly laughed. "There are always people around. How could they?"

"No one's here at night."

"But you're here."

"When I'm over there scrubbing the pools."

"But he's home every night," Xiaoli said to herself.

"The second of last month, when your niece, Banjiu, was sick, you went back to Niu Village and spent a night there." Xin inched closer. "Remember?"

She nodded when she recalled what had happened.

"I went over to scrub the pools that night, as usual. Then I got hungry, so I came back here for something to eat and heard some noise before I walked in. At first, I thought it might be a thief, and I was scared. I'm short and not strong enough to fight anyone, so I didn't walk in. Instead, I peeked in through the door and was shocked to see your husband and Qi Yafen doing you-know-what. They were naked, doing it on this table. I didn't want any trouble, so I sneaked back to the bathhouse. I didn't want to tell you because she was still working here. Turns out she's an ingrate, so I decided to expose her."

Xiaoli felt her head buzz. Flipping over the table to which Xin had pointed, she stormed out the door to go see Feng at his shop in town. She was barely out the door when she realized she'd left her cell phone behind, so she turned to go back inside, where she saw Xin in the corner, snickering, his hand over his mouth. Now she knew that it was her husband, not Yafen, Xin had wanted to expose. She also realized that, like Qi Yafen with her diner, Xin had just taken his revenge. She was impressed by their patience, if nothing else. But she had no time to deal with Xin now; she raced out the door and headed for the repair shop.

3

Niu Xiaoli strode through town and arrived at the shop. Feng was on the floor working on a motor scooter, his hands greasy, parts strewn around him. She walked in and, without a word, pulled down the rolling door, so startling Feng that he jumped to his feet.

"What are you doing? It's not closing time yet."

"I need to talk you in private."

"What is it?" he asked, crossing his arms.

She came straight to the point after dragging a stool over to sit by the door.

"What's going on between you and Qi Yafen?"

Feng froze and stared back at her.

"What do you mean? I don't understand."

Despite his answer, Xiaoli detected a hint of panic on his face, which convinced her she was right.

"You don't understand? Then let me be clear. When did you start having sex with her?"

"Having sex?" Feng said wide-eyed. "She's my sister's schoolmate, and five years older than me. Who told you that?"

"Old Xin," Xiaoli said. "He saw you together one night."

Feng wiped his hands on a rag as he started toward the door.

"He's lying. I'm going to find him and toss him into the river."

But the door was down, and Xiaoli was sitting by it. She pointed to another stool.

"Sit down."

He sat down to await the interrogation, but she sat quietly, with no more questions. He did not dare bring up anything, so they sat silently, saying nothing for a couple of hours. It was getting dark outside and dim inside the shop. He broke the silence:

"It's getting dark. Time to open the diner for night business."

"I don't want the diner anymore." She added, "Don't think about leaving if you don't come clean."

"I did. I told you nothing's going on between us." He stomped his foot angrily.

"We'll keep sitting here then."

So they did. She turned on the lights when it was completely dark out. Two hours later, hunger pangs had him checking his watch; it was ten o'clock.

"Aren't you hungry?" he asked her.

"Of course."

"Let's get something to eat."

"We'll go after you tell me everything."

"I have nothing to tell. Do you want me to make something up?"

"Then we'll keep sitting here," she proclaimed.

So, they did, until after midnight, when his belly was crying out for food. His stomach had been acting up the previous noon, so he'd had only had a bowl of thin soup without noodles. Going without food for hours made his stomach act up differently, and it felt like it was pressed up against his backbone. When he was eight years old, he'd had a fight with a schoolmate and hurt the boy's head with a brick. Afraid his father would beat him over the fight, he didn't dare return home and had to go without food, an experience he hadn't had to repeat until now. He was able to put up with the hunger during the night, but the arrival of dawn brought the sensation of insects crawling, biting, and shouting angrily in his stomach, their little heads raised. Feng looked at Xiaoli, who stared back at him with a calm, impassive expression, so he swallowed and remained on his stool. It was getting light out, and rays of sun gradually seeped in through the windows. The shop's rolling door was still down, giving the impression that Feng was taking the day off, so no one came. By noon, the hunger pangs were gone, which, he knew, was caused by the numbing effect of starvation. But thirst replaced hunger, as he realized he'd not had a drop of water since the previous afternoon. His mouth felt dry when he wasn't thinking about being thirsty, but now that he was, it felt as if every cell in his body was parched. Hunger had been hard, but thirst was ten times worse. By that afternoon, he felt that the insects were not only gnawing at his nerves and cells, but they were also sucking away every last bit of moisture in him. He was like a towel with the last drop of water wrung out; his head felt scorched, while his body turned into a bundle of dry kindling that threatened to burst into flames. He touched his lips to feel them covered in blisters, so were Xiaoli's when he checked. But she kept her eyes on him, with the same calm composure. Finally, he sighed.

"I can take it, but I don't want you to suffer, so I'll tell you."

"Go ahead."

"Something is going on between Qi Yafen and me."

"When did it start?"

"Five years ago."

Xiaoli felt a loud clap go off in her head, not because of the affair but because of the timeline. She'd thought it had started recently, but it turned out it had been much longer. Xiaoli and Jinhua had just started seeing each other five years before. She'd liked him because she thought he was reliable; she never imagined that he would get involved with her while sleeping with Qi at the same time. Furthermore, Qi Yafen had been married at the time and had only gotten a divorce three years before, making her an adulteress. What a disgusting pair of cheats, she cursed silently.

"She's five years older than you and she was married when you started sleeping with her," she said. "What do you get out of it?"

Feng thought the question over and said, "She's creative in bed."

Xiaoli was shocked. Qi had looked so quiet and reserved; who could have guessed she would be a creative lover? It occurred to her that Feng had been creative in bed when they started seeing each other and could make it last an hour, which was one of the reasons she'd decided to marry him. Obviously, he'd learned it from Qi. So, if they were creative, then it could only mean that Xiaoli was not. She was on the verge of tears.

"Since you liked her creativity in bed, why didn't you marry her? Why did you start seeing me?"

"She was married at the time."

"Then why didn't you marry her three years ago, when she got her divorce?"

"She has a kid. I just want to have some fun. I don't want to marry her."

"Now I understand why you began ignoring me at night a year into our marriage."

"That's not it." Feng waved the accusation away.

That reminded her of something.

"You could do it anywhere, so why did you do it in my diner last month?"

Feng looked down and did not respond. She picked up a motor scooter part and flung it at him. He dodged before muttering:

"She said it was exciting to do it there; it helped vent her hatred."

Xiaoli had to wonder how much hatred Qi had harbored against her. It appeared it was not simply because Xiaoli's diner had forced her stand out of business. Qi could have believed that Xiaoli had taken Feng from her. Then something else occurred to her, and so she asked:

"So, you and she had talked about opening another diner to compete with me then?"

"I actually told her not to do it. It'd be too obvious, but she wouldn't listen." Feng waved it off again but continued softly, "She can be stubborn sometimes."

To Xiaoli, Qi Yafen was not stubborn, just vicious. She stood up and pulled the rolling door open; the bright sunlight poured in and blinded them. She looked at him.

"I want a divorce. Not because of your affair, but because of your affair with someone who hates me. And not because you lied to me, but because you cheated on me five years ago. Actually, it's not even because you cheated five years ago, but because you continued to cheat on me after we got married."

She stormed out of the shop.

4

The civil affairs clerk at the township office was a short, balding man in his forties. Old Gu had handled the paperwork a year earlier, when Niu Xiaoli and Feng Jinhua were married. After she opened the diner, he often stopped by at noon for a bowl of soup.

"Why do you want a divorce?" he asked.

Before coming to the office, Feng had begged Xiaoli not to expose his affair with Qi Yafen. Xiaoli had agreed for reasons of her own.

"I won't tell anyone, not because of you, but because of myself. I don't want to lose face. I don't want to look like a fool."

"You're right," Feng said, but immediately regretted opening his mouth.

"I won't tell the truth, so you'll have to lie for us. I won't say a word at the office," said Xiaoli.

Feng had to agree, which was why he answered Gu's question.

"We don't get along."

"Everyone says that when they come to get a divorce," Gu said with a frown. "It's too vague. I need something more concrete."

"I'll give you something concrete then," Feng replied, after a glance at Xiaoli. "We started arguing yesterday afternoon, and we're still fighting this afternoon. We had nothing to eat or drink for twenty-four hours, and we nearly died from hunger and thirst. Just look at the blisters on our lips."

Gu nodded after checking their lips.

"That's a good reason, when lives are involved. Have you decided what to do with your property?"

"We have two businesses. I own a motor scooter repair shop, and she has a diner. We've agreed that I'll take the shop, and she'll hold on to the diner. We'll keep what we make from our individual business."

"That's the advantage of running individual businesses," Gu said with a nod, before bringing out two divorce forms from a drawer. He was about to fill them in when the phone rang.

"Hold on. My boss wants to see me," he said after answering the phone. He left and returned five minutes later.

"You'll have to wait on the divorce."

"Why?" Xiaoli was unhappy.

"You need to clear up something first," Gu said.

"What have I done?" Feng was startled.

"Not you, her." Gu pointed to Xiaoli, who froze, as did Feng.

"What has she done?"

Two men and a woman walked in. One of the men, named Liu, was from the local police station, but the other two were strangers. All three looked visibly relieved when they saw Xiaoli.

"We've been looking for you all day. The diner is closed, and so is the repair shop. We thought you'd run off," Liu said to Xiaoli as he pointed at the other two, "They're from the Public Security Bureau of another province; they want to talk to you."

The two strangers did not look menacing. The woman studied Xiaoli's face before pronouncing, "That's her. I'm sure. Just like the one in the videos."

"She does look a bit like a Westerner," the man said after a closer look at Xiaoli.

"I'm afraid you'll have to come with us," the woman said while taking out her badge to show Xiaoli.

"Why?" Xiaoli felt a minor panic rising.

"You know what you did in our capital city."

This sounded bad. Feng spoke up for Xiaoli even though they were about to get a divorce. "You must have it wrong. She's never been there."

"Ask her if she's been there." The man sneered.

"You can't lie your way out of this. We've got Su Shuang," the woman added.

Xiaoli blanched, but she told the police:

"No need to say more. I'll go with you." She then turned to Gu. "Are we divorced, Old Gu?"

"Not yet. We didn't have time to get it filed."

"So, we're still married." Xiaoli turned back to the woman, "Can I have a few words with my husband before I go with you?"

The woman looked at the man, who in turned surveyed the window and nodded when he noticed the steel bars. Everyone left the room to wait outside, leaving Xiaoli with Feng, who stammered in shock, "When, when did you go to that city? How, how come I didn't know? What did you do there?"

"Forget that. I want to ask you something."

"What?" Feng asked dumbly.

"I'm leaving with them, so can you deliver a message for me? For the fact that we've been married for a year, if not for anything else."

"What?"

She put her arms around him and put her mouth over his. Feng was surprised before realizing that she had taken something out of her pocket and pressed it into his hand. It felt like a bankcard; he understood what was going on and quickly stashed it in his pocket. His lips hurt and, seeing hers bloodied, sensed that his were too. The blisters on their lips had burst during the kiss. She inched her bloody lips up to his ear and whispered:

"The account contains the 900,000 yuan the diner made last year. I was thinking about opening another one at the rear entrance to compete with Qi Yafen, but that's not going to happen now.

"You take the card to my brother and tell him the pass code is Banjiu's birthday. I want him to keep 20,000 yuan for Banjiu's education and the rest for him to buy another wife."

5

The police took Xiaoli away. It felt just like a year before, when they were on a rural bus traveling to the county town before switching to a municipal bus bound for the city, or when they were in a taxi heading from the bus depot to the train station, where she heard the train whistle. That had been exactly how she'd made the trip with Zhu Juhua and Little Monkey to look for Song Caixia. Nothing about the travel or the scenery seemed all that different; even the sounds were familiar. Except for her travel companions, that is. Zhu and her son had been replaced by the police. On one hand, it felt like only yesterday, but on the other hand, so much had happened over the past year that it might as well have been a lifetime ago. As they waited for their train, the police took her to a stall to the south of the station for some mutton soup and fried bread. The year before, she and Zhu and her son had mutton soup at the same stall. They had not ordered any bread, though, since Zhu had brought some with her. It was the same owner, an overweight man with a thin moustache and a white cap. The price of the soup had gone up, from three yuan a bowl to four. As they ate, Xiaoli spotted a couplet pasted by the door of a store selling roast chickens: "Business grows and spreads to the four seas/Wealth increases and flows like the three rivers." Over the door was another line: "Gold pours in daily." It was the seventh month of the lunar year, which meant the couplets had been up for that long. They were tattered and faded, the bottom half fluttering in the wind. She recalled that she had the exact same couplets on the door of her diner back home, where diners had crowded into her shop the day before. She felt like crying when she realized how much had changed in one day.

6

A preliminary hearing for Xiaoli was held at a police station. It was not the same policewoman who had escorted her from her hometown. The one earlier was in her thirties, while the current one was middle-aged. Before they started, she made Xiaoli watch several videos, which showed her having sex with different men. In the video clips, she was naked, as were the men, some tall and some short, some fat and some skinny, some lasting longer and some finishing quickly, some in front and some from the back, some lying down and some standing, some kissing her all over and some having her kiss them all over. When she was done, the policewoman froze the frame and looked at her.

"Is that you in the video clips, Niu Xiaoli?"

Xiaoli stared back at the woman wordlessly.

"You were called Song Caixia back then, weren't you?"

Xiaoli continued to stare without responding.

"Do you know who these men are?"

Still not a word from Xiaoli.

"Did you know why these videos were taken?"

Xiaoli remained silent. The policewoman pointed at the computer screen before banging on the desk.

"We have all the evidence and witnesses. Lying isn't going to work."

"Who took the videos?" Xiaoli finally asked.

"I'm the one asking questions, not you," the woman snapped after a pause.

"Who took the videos?" Xiaoli persisted.

"Answer my question first."

"I won't tell you if you don't tell me first," Xiaoli said stubbornly.

The policewoman sized her up before finally saying:

"All right. I'll tell you. It was a real estate developer named Fu."

Xiaoli considered the information and recalled the man. On the first day she arrived in the provincial capital with Su Shuang, they had had hot pot at the diner by the river. In the private dining room, she'd met Fu, a middle-aged, bald man with donkey's face. Su Shuang had told her that Fu owned a garment factory, but later she said he was a real estate developer who was worth billions, making money from building all the houses in the city. Fu had then paid for Su to present Xiaoli as a virgin so she could have sex with lots of men. Xiaoli had asked about these men and was told that they were all men who were more powerful and wealthier than Fu. Xiaoli had agreed to do it ten times, but later she'd added two more on her own, convinced that she could go back home with 120,000 yuan, never to see Su and Fu again. That had been what Su had told her. She never imagined that Fu would set up a video camera in the room? She recalled the room in a traditional courtyard called B18, located in a suburb of the capital city. She'd have preferred death if she'd known there had been a video camera recording everything. There had been two other girls in the private dining room. She remembered one of them was called Wang Jinghong and the other Li Boqin, both of whom had joked about Fu's baldness and donkey face. Fu could not get a word out because of his stutter, when the girls launched another round of verbal assaults. He could barely fend them off, let alone fight back. At the time, Xiaoli had thought he was a nice man with a good temper, but now she knew he was as vicious as a viper, with his secret video camera. She would die if the clips got out.

"Why did he video tape me?"

"It wasn't to tape you," the woman said.

"What for then?"

"To blackmail the men in the video."

"Why did he do that?"

"They're all rich and powerful men. Fu had dealings with them and was afraid they might sell him out."

Now Xiaoli understood the purpose behind Fu's video clips. She did not know if Fu had succeeded in his blackmail, but he had put her in jeopardy. Xiaoli almost felt like laughing.

"Blackmail or not, it's between them. What do you want with me?"

"It's not that simple." The policewoman snickered.

"What do you mean?"

"He made the video for blackmailing, and we'll charge him for extortion. You participated in the process of making these indecent clips, and that makes you an accomplice. We could charge you with blackmail and extortion too."

Reminded of Wang Jinghong and Li Boqin, Xiaoli asked:

"Fu had two more women working for him. Will they be charged with the same crime?"

"They're prostitutes. That's against the law, but they won't be charged." The woman shook her head.

"Why is that?"

"Fu didn't videotape them."

"Why did he pick me?" Xiaoli said bitterly.

"Because you were sleeping with officials, even with a governor."

Xiaoli was shaken. She had only known that she slept with several men, some tall and some short, some fat and some skinny, some lasting longer and some finishing up fast, some in front and some from the back, and some lying down and some standing. She had also known these were powerful and rich men, but it never occurred to her that they were officials, including a governor.

"Besides the governor, there were also two mayors, several bank directors, as well as the chief of a county highway bureau. They've all been put under double discipline. If you cooperate and help us out, you'll get a lighter sentence."

"I didn't do anything to Fu, so why did he pick me to sleep with these officials?" Xiaoli asked, bewildered.

"Maybe because you're prettier than the others." The woman finally smiled. "Or because you look like a Westerner."

Xiaoli didn't know what to say.

"Will you cooperate and help us out?"

"I have one more question."

"What is it?"

"I called myself Song Caixia when I was here last year, so how did you find me?"

"Where were you staying back then?"

"In a hotel."

"Who were you with?"

"Su Shuang."

"What do you need to check into a hotel?" the policewoman asked.

Xiaoli's ID card was the cause of her downfall, that plus Su Shuang, who had been arrested.

"Su Shuang told us she made you out to be a virgin each time. Is that true?"

Xiaoli had to own up to it, now that it had come to this, so she nodded.

"Are you a virgin?"

Xiaoli shook her head.

"Strictly speaking, what you did was also an extortion of sorts."

She turned the computer screen around, pecked at the keyboard, and turned the screen around so that it was facing Xiaoli. On it was a frontal shot of a man in his fifties, with fair skin, hair combed back, wearing gold-rimmed glasses. Xiaoli recognized the man right away, her first client at B18.

"What did this man say to you at the time?"

Xiaoli recalled that their conversation was all conducted in bed, but she could not recall anything specific after a year, except the lies she had told the man, who had believed every word. Unable to recall anything the man said to her, Xiaoli nevertheless racked her brain until she finally blurted out:

"Oh dear."

It was not the answer the confounded policewoman was waiting for.

Appendix I

In early September, the headlines on major websites across the country were about how a woman had brought down twelve officials in two provinces. They had slept with the same woman, who called herself Song Caixia, but her real name was Niu Xiaoli. Everyone referred to her as Song Caixia, however, because that had been the name she used when sleeping with these officials, and no one remembered her real name. As one of the officials was Li Anbang, a provincial governor, the explosive nature of the affair had the power of atomic fission and shook up the whole country; the name Song Caixia became an Internet sensation overnight and overshadowed the news of a meeting among three dozen heads of state that would take place in Beijing three days later.

The news had drawn hundreds of posts, some hurling invectives against prostitutes, some against the corrupt officials, some against the darkness in society, while yet others praised Song Caixia. A ditty, "Song of Caixia" began to circulate among those on her side:

> *You came down from the bed,*
> *The springtide, your graceful bearing,*
> *You ran up to the corrupt officials,*
> *Casually untying your pants;*
> *You used your sweet flowing milk,*
> *Nursing a team of public servants;*
> *Your surging, billowing waves,*
> *Submerged the head of a governor;*
> *We all sing the praise of Caixia,*
> *Fight corruption like plucking greens;*

We adore and admire Caixia,
You are a rare talent no one has ever seen.

There was also the citation for an award that went viral on WeChat:

Award citation for a Saint

She's a virgin who slept with twelve officials; with a bedsheet alone she exposed a major corruption case; her earnings came from her labor alone, but caused the corrupt officials to lose millions; she is not agent 007, but she braved the tiger's den to catch the enemy; she fought alone, but behind her stand tens of thousands of us, people who talk without lifting a finger.

She's a saint, and her name is Song Caixia.

Someone even created a diagram to illustrate the order in which she slept with the officials and probed the connections between them, with the conclusion that the cases broke one by one, thanks largely to Song Caixia, but also to the poorly made firecrackers on the truck driving over the Number Three Rainbow Bridge over the Caihong River. If the firecrackers had been better made, they would not have gone off on their own. If they had not, then nothing else would have happened. The chief of the county highway bureau—the famous Mr. Smiley Face and Mr. Watch-Face—was brought down by poorly made firecrackers, as he implicated Li Anbang and others. It is common for minor officials to be embroiled in their superiors' problems, but it is rare for it to be the other way around; oftentimes only those with direct supervisory authority are enmeshed in each other's troubles, but it is uncommon among total strangers. The explosion of a truckload of low-quality firecrackers drew together people who had nothing to do with one another. Someone completed an online search and found that the firecrackers came from a factory called Blazing Colorful Firecrackers and Fireworks Manufacturer LTD. Upon the discovery, Netizens started giving tips and sending award banners to the company's web site. The most common term of praise on the banners was: Fuckin' A.

Appendix I

Internet supervisors removed the news items and threads. Netizens would have lost interest in two days if they'd been left online, but instead they popped up in Moments, where they were passed around, precisely because they had been taken down.

Appendix II

On the second day after the Song Caixia incident went public, Zhao Pingfan, who had fled to the United States because of his connections to Li Anbang, talked about the case in a radio interview in New York. According to Zhao, Li's arrest was not simply because of corruption; in fact, he was the victim of a political power struggle. Li's province had been the base of a certain individual who had recently suffered a downfall. Li had taken over as governor, with the man's recommendation, which made Li his lackey in his enemy's eyes, even though Li had not known him beforehand. Their contact started only after Li became the governor, roughly a year before. Li was nothing but an innocent bystander, collateral damage, in the aftermath of the Song Caixia incident. The official reason of his arrest was corruption. Zhao continued, corruption in China is a problem with no solution. Corrupt officials can be arrested, but no one can guarantee that those who remain are blameless. He followed up with shady details from his dealings with Beijing and local officials in his real estate developments over three decades. He even named names, some of them high officials, expanding on how officials colluded with businessmen and double-crossed each other for profit. A case in point: two years earlier, someone at the highest level of the Chinese government, using state apparatus, extorted over 10 billion yuan from him; yet he remained in his current position and had made several high-profile purchases of businesses in Europe the month before. The interview was aired in a prime-time slot—eight to ten at night. The two-hour program was broadcast live on many Chinese web sites in the United States and viewed by many Chinese living there. Someone left a comment later saying it was an attack by one scoundrel on another, like a dogfight or a farce. Another one countered that it was a credible story precisely because one scoundrel had lashed out against another. Someone else joined in to say that for Zhao Pingfan to use the Song Caixia incident to speak up was not a mere farce to help Li or to offer inside details. Most likely it was for self-preservation. He was implicated in Li's case and in possession of substantial evidence of his dealings with many officials, so he knew he was in danger. He needed to talk to show he was still alive; that way, people would notice when he disappeared. The louder he talked, the safer he would be. If he had not taken this opportunity to make his voice heard, he might vanish from the world one day without anyone knowing about it. Yet another reader commented on how comical it was that a powerful real estate tycoon had to speak up for self-preservation, getting a free ride on the coattails of a prostitute.

The recorded interview spread in China through WeChat, without notable reactions. It had a total lifespan of five minutes online before Internet censors took it down. In the meantime, a team of paparazzi turned up scandalous news of a female star's affair, which would not have warranted any space if not for the fact that the affair was with a shemale from Thailand, making her the headline on every major website. Under such circumstances, Zhao might as well not have spoken, and the comical effect was all for naught.

Part Two

Afterword:
Everyone You Know

One year later.

PART THREE

MAIN STORY: FOOT BATH

1

Shortly before May 1st, International Labor Day, Ma Zhongcheng was promoted to the position of Deputy Chief of a certain city's environmental protection bureau. It was so unexpected that Ma's blood pressure shot up at the announcement. He had been a section head in the bureau, one of eleven, so he had assumed he would never have been chosen to be the deputy. Keeping to himself and doing his job dutifully, he had been biding his time till the day he could retire in one piece.

Earlier that year, one of the deputy chiefs retired and left his post vacant, turning the office upside down when all the section heads jostled to replace him. They named names, snitching on each other. For members of the disciplinary committee, their offices became a home away from home. As soon as one case was adjudicated, another letter would be delivered to bring the members back. Since no one was squeaky clean, every informant's letter produced results, and every informant was informed on. Ma stayed out of the fray and was thus spared because no one had expected him to be a competitor. Once the office was turned upside down, Ma Zhongcheng, who had stayed out of the infighting, became the accidental beneficiary. He did not say a word when the bureau chief gave him the news, not because he had nothing to say but because it was so sudden, and his blood pressure spiked. It was not until he got home that he spread his hands and said to his wife:

"Am I good and talented enough to get this?"

"You are not. But you have good and talented people to thank for it." His wife added, "Isn't this just a case of the fisherman reaping the benefit of a fight between a sandpiper and a clam? Don't let it go to your head, Old Ma."

Ma kept quiet as his blood pressure returned to normal. The whole family was happy, since a promotion is, after all, good news. His son, a high school student, suggested a celebration for the promotion and for Labor Day, a sort of double happiness. Fine. But how? His daughter, who was in middle school, wanted a family trip over the weeklong holiday. Where to? After an animated discussion, the four of them came up with three possibilities: the best, a trip to SMT (Singapore, Malaysia, and Thailand); the middle, to a domestic tourist spot, and the basic, a feast of carp at a restaurant on the Yellow River, thirty li away.

To save time and trouble, Ma's wife voted for the carp feast, which their children deemed insufficient for the occasion. She then changed her tune; a riverside dinner might not be enough, but a trip to SMT was out of the question. It would cost over 7,000 yuan per person, which came to more than 30,000 yuan for the whole family. Too expensive. As for domestic spots, they had been to Mount Tai, Mount Hua, Jiuzhaigou, Chengde, and the Bashang Grassland, separately. Their son came up with the idea of visiting the Sea Goddess Statue. A newly created tourist attraction in a southern province, it was an imitation of New York's Statue of Liberty, with a sculpture of a woman holding a torch on the beach. The new site had been popular among tourists because of the many discounts.

They decided that was where they would go.

Main Story: Foot Bath

2

So there they were. On the first day, they went to see the statue and the ocean, where they swam, except Ma's wife, who did not know how to swim and stayed on the beach to people-watch. On the second day, they visited World Park, the Aquarium, and the amusement park, where they enjoyed the rollercoaster and flume rides. Ma had not wanted to ride the rollercoaster because of elevated blood pressure, but their tickets were a package deal, and it would be a waste if he did not go. At his daughter's urging, he sat down with his eyes shut and came out unaffected after all the ups and downs.

"That's strange," Ma commented.

For lunch that day they picked out a seafood restaurant that specialized in mantis shrimps. As she peeled a shrimp, Ma's wife said:

"The Sea Goddess Statue wasn't as big a deal as I expected, and the rides were just thrown together.

"They weren't very well constructed, but we got a discount at all of them."

Meanwhile, their children had made plans for the rest of their vacation: a hot springs bath, grass skiing, sand surfing, a hot air balloon ride, scuba diving, and dolphin watching on a fishing boat, which led to an argument about what to do when. A chirping sound on Ma's cell phone alerted him to a text, which stunned him into silence after he read it. The bureau chief wanted him to return as soon as possible; something terrible had happened to Old Liang, the other deputy chief, who was on duty over the holiday: his mother had died of a heart attack that morning. The news affected everyone in the family.

"It's so disappointing," his wife said.

"What's the point of being deputy chief?" Ma complained, if I can't even enjoy myself when I'm a thousand li away?"

But it was a summons from his boss; besides, Old Liang's mother had died. For both professional and personal reasons, Ma had to return. The family talked it over and decided that, under such circumstances, they had to split up. The three of them would stay to enjoy the rest of their trip, so the expense would not go to waste, while Ma would go home alone.

"Never a day off for an official," Ma said with a sigh. "See you next time, Sea Goddess."

3

With his backpack over his shoulder, Ma Zhongcheng took a bus into the capital, where he hailed a taxi for the train station. After buying his ticket, he felt hungry, so he walked out of the lobby and ordered a bowl of noodles at a diner across from the station square. His hunger satisfied, he sat down on a flowerbed to people-watch. A skinny man walked up and said to him:

"How about a bath for your tired feet, Elder Brother?"

Ma knew he was a pimp, so he said:

"I don't have time for that."

"You sound like you're from out of town, Elder Brother. Since you've traveled so far to get here, why not have a girl to talk to?"

Ma shook his head.

"Our footbath is right over there, not far."

Ma shook his head again.

"Our girls are real beauties."

Ma checked his cell phone and saw that his train would not leave for three hours. I have to wait anyway, he said to himself. It's a holiday and I got a promotion, so I ought to give myself a good time.

"Is it safe?" Ma asked.

"Absolutely." Skinny added, "And not just for your sake. You'll be gone after this one time, but our girls have to do it every day."

Ma had to agree, so he got to his feet.

4

Skinny led Ma to a spot behind the train station, more secluded and quieter than the square, where they turned into an alley; a barber pole marked the footbath. A woman in her fifties wearing tights greeted him with a smile.

"Come in, Elder Brother. Have a seat and a cup of tea."

Skinny walked out while the woman poured hot water from a drinking fountain into a paper cup and handed it to Ma.

"Would you like the minor or the major service?"

Ma knew the minor service meant regular massage, while the major one offered something additional.

"I'll have to see what she looks like first," Ma said while blowing away tealeaves in his cup.

The woman smiled and shouted at the back of the room:

"Come on out, Little Cui. You've got a client."

A woman parted the curtain and came out. Despite the "Little" in her name, she was clearly way into her fifties. When she smiled, bits of powder fell from her wrinkled, heavily made-up face, to Ma's great disappointment.

"Her?" Ma added, "How about someone else?"

"The others are all called out," Woman in tights said.

"Then forget it." Ma stood up, but the woman blocked his way,

"A younger one will be back soon. Can you wait?"

"How long?" Ma asked.

"Not too long. Two hours at most."

Ma checked the clock on the wall. It was two and half hours before his train left; if he waited for two hours, he would have half an hour left, just enough time to return to the station. He could not wait that long, so he turned to walk out, but the woman stopped him again and pointed at Little Cui.

"She may look old, but she offers great service." She added, "She has lots of experience because she's older. Besides, she's cheaper than the younger ones."

Ma sized up Little Cui again. Despite her age, she did have a pleasant face. Her midsection was in good enough shape to show rounded buttocks. He realized after a closer scrutiny she had the charm of an older woman.

"How much cheaper?" Ma asked, still undecided.

"Major or minor service?"

"I just want a foot bath."

"A young one will cost you 50 yuan, but thirty for her."

5

Little Cui took Ma to a room and brought hot water in a wooden basin for his footbath. As he soaked his feet before the bath, she massaged his legs and feet, starting with the calves, then the thighs, where her hands continued to travel up to his crotch.

"How about a major service, Elder Brother?" she asked.

"I told you I didn't want that."

"It's holiday time, so why not do it, Elder Brother?"

Ma checked her again. The creases on her face were even more noticeable at close range. He wondered about doing it with a woman in her fifties and how dry she might be down there. No reaction on his part either. As if she could tell what he was thinking, she said:

"How about an oral service if you don't want the major one? I'm good at everything."

The mention of oral sex had Ma's heart race. She might be dry down there, but not up here. Ma's wife was a bit of a shrew and, with their children grown, they had not shared any physical intimacy in five years. He felt something stir down below, so he asked:

"How much?"

"Same as the major service, 300 yuan. I'm sure you know, Elder Brother, that oral service is harder."

"Too expensive. Not for me."

"How much do you want to pay?"

"One hundred yuan."

"Ask around and you won't find anyone doing it for a hundred yuan anywhere in China." She laughed before adding, "Let's not haggle over this, Elder Brother. Two hundred yuan. You're my first client of the day, so it's a good omen for me."

Ma did not say anything, which meant silent consent, so she reached out.

"You need to pay up first, Elder Brother."

"I'll pay when it's done. I'm good for it."

"Business first, so we won't argue later," she said with a smile.

Ma opened his backpack, took out his wallet, and counted out 200 yuan. She stashed the money in her bra before wiping his feet dry.

"I'll be right back, Elder Brother."

He lay down on the bed and she returned after a while with two cups of water, one of them steamy, and a pack of moist towelettes. After placing them on a bedside chest, she took off his pants and wiped him down with the towelettes; she asked him to raise his buttocks for her to wipe him in the back. He felt something stirring down below again. When she took a condom out from her bra to put on him, he stopped her.

"Who wears a condom for oral service?"

"I have canker sores, Elder Brother, and I don't want to give them to you."

He had to let her put the condom on. Then she picked up one of the cups and had a sip of the warm water before taking him in her mouth and moving her tongue around. After spitting out the warm water, she changed to cool water; the change in temperature excited him so much he was shaking and had a full-blown erection. She spat out the water, raised his buttocks, and licked him all over, as he felt himself transported to heaven. This woman in her fifties was different and the right one for him; she was worth the money. It had been a long time since he'd last had such an experience. She moved to the front, put him in her mouth again, and moved so fast that he came with a loud cry. He was panting hard as he lay limp on the bed when the door was kicked open and four burly guys stormed in.

"Police!" the one in front shouted.

Ma was flabbergasted. He quickly regained his composure and jumped out of bed to flee, but they grabbed him and pushed him to the floor.

6

Ma was taken out of the footbath and pushed into a van, along with Little Cui and the woman in tights. One of the policemen tossed Ma's backpack in after them.

Main Story: Foot Bath

Ten minutes later they arrived in a yard, which Ma thought was the police station, until he saw the sign, Station Joint Defense Team. The four men were in plain clothes, which told him that they were not policemen, but members of the neighborhood defense team. When the three of them were pushed out of the van, the two women were taken into one room, while Ma was led into another. One of the defense team members stood Ma against a wall as soon they walked in and searched him, while the other one checked his backpack. A third man, a stumpy, fat one, came in holding a teacup. He blew into it as the others called out, "Boss."

Their boss sized Ma up and asked:

"What did he do?"

"Whoring."

"I did not," Ma shot back.

One of the men threw a sheet of crumpled newspaper onto the desk and opened it to show the condom.

"Here's the evidence. Would you like us to do a DNA test?"

"I had an oral service; you can't count that as whoring," Ma argued.

"That was what Clinton said years ago, but the US court considered it the same as having sex."

The man checking the backpack took out Ma's ID cards.

"Hey, he's not just anybody."

"What do you mean?" the other one asked.

"He's a government official, a deputy bureau chief."

Their boss took the ID from him and asked, after examining it:

"Do you know what happens to a government official traveling away from home who visits a prostitute?"

"You're not the police. You don't have the authority to arrest me," Ma said, recalling the sign at the entrance.

"Don't you worry. This is only the first stop. We'll send you to the police station shortly," one of them said.

"Nothing serious will happen there." The other one followed up. "Two weeks of detention, and your work unit and family will be notified, of course."

A cold sweat broke out on Ma's back. Two weeks of detention meant his work unit would put him under double discipline. He'd be a laughingstock immediately after his promotion. And his family. His wife was such a shrew that he would die at her hands once she heard the news; even if he managed to survive, it would be about the same as living in a detention center. These would not be the worst consequences actually; the worst outcome would be the effect on his children, who would likely stop going to school. And when the news spread and everyone in town knew that Ma Zhongcheng had been put under double discipline because of prostitution, how and where would he live? Losing his confidence, Ma pled with the boss:

"How about a different solution, Boss?"

"What do you have in mind?" The boss looked at him.

"I can pay a fine."

"Don't be in such a hurry. You'll have to pay a fine, in addition to detention, once we send you to the police station," one man said.

Ma turned to him and pled:

"What I mean is, I'll pay a fine here and you let me go."

"We're law enforcement." Their boss sounded upset. "This isn't a game. Take him away."

The two men came up to grab Ma, who tried one more time:

"This is my first offense, Elder Brothers. Please give me a chance." He continued, "I have parents and children. How can I go on living if everyone knows about this? I'd have to hang myself."

He slumped to the floor and, with his arms wrapped around the desk legs, refused to leave. The two men had to stop dragging him.

"He looks wimpy enough to be a first-time offender," one of them said to their boss. "Should we give him another chance?"

"Yes, he does look wimpy. He might just hang himself if the news spread," the other joined in.

"I will. I will hang myself." Ma promised promptly.

"The government is advocating humane law enforcement," one of them said.

Their boss considered the situation as he looked at Ma slumped on the floor.

"This won't be easy," he said.

The man's pause was a silent consent to Ma, who bowed to him.

"Thank you, thank you so much, Boss."

One of the men kicked him.

"So, how big a fine do you think you should pay?"

"However much I have in the backpack."

The man opened his wallet and counted. "Twenty-four hundred yuan."

Ma got to his feet and said timidly:

"Can I have a little for travel?"

"This isn't a business deal." The boss slammed his cup down on the desk. "Take him to the police station."

"All right. I won't need anything."

"You shouldn't have said that," one of the men chided Ma as he pointed to a bankcard in the wallet. "Isn't this a bank card?"

Taking the wallet, Ma got his ID back, picked up his backpack, and ran toward the door, where he stopped to look at the three men.

"Changed your mind? Would you prefer the police station?"

"Can I have that?" Ma pointed at the condom on the desk.

"It's evidence. We have to keep it, so you won't make a false accusation against us in the future." One of the men banged on the desk.

"All right. You can have it," Ma said diffidently, spun around and fled.

7

Ma Zhongcheng returned to the train station and sat on the flowerbed to catch his breath. What just happened felt like a dream; the event was frightening, and he'd nearly had to hang himself. Luckily, he'd emerged unscathed, despite the scare. He'd lost over 2,000 yuan, but he had gained peace in return, suffering a financial loss to prevent a disaster. As he considered the outcome, he had to say that the joint defense team was kind and reasonable, for they didn't try to extort him after fining him 2,400 yuan. He would have had to comply if they'd told him to withdraw another 10,000 or 20,000 yuan from an ATM since he could not lose face and his job over that amount of money.

After he calmed down, Ma took out his train ticket, knowing that it had left without him. He retrieved his bankcard from the wallet in the backpack and withdrew 1,000 yuan from an ATM so he could change his ticket. He paid the difference and got a new ticket for the next train, which would not leave for three hours. With no place to go and his fear still lingering, he went back to the square. He wondered about the two women who had been arrested along with him; what had happened to Little Cui and the woman in tights? Maybe they had suffered the same treatment as he had, having to pay a fine, or maybe they'd been sent to the police station. The three of them had suffered the same fate, even though they had not known each other until that day; they had been the cause of Ma's misfortune, or he had been theirs. If he hadn't visited the footbath, they wouldn't have been arrested. Feeling emotional over the situation, he got up and headed to the rear of the station. He wanted to see what had happened to the two women. Naturally, he wouldn't step through the door. He would look from a distance. They had arrested him inside, but they couldn't possibly do that when he was out on the street, could they? Ma was astounded to see the post still twirling outside and that the bath was lit inside. He walked past the station and turned into the alley. So, the bath remained open. But how could that be when it had just been raided? How did they have the nerve to keep it open after what had just happened? Something fishy was going on, Ma decided. He wanted to go inside to ask but could not shake off the fright from his recent arrest, so he stayed where he was and kept his eyes on the bath. The skinny man who had talked him into visiting the bath walked out and headed his way. Ma ducked behind a wall and began trailing him once he was out on the main street. He went up and tapped him on the shoulder when they reached a grove of trees at a pocket park, with no one in sight.

"I need to talk to you, pal."

Skinny turned to check Ma out. He was surprised, but quickly regained his composure.

"Who are you? I don't know you."

"Oh, yes you do." Ma grabbed his arm.

"Let go." Skinny wriggled. "Trying to rob me? I'll shout."

"No, I'm not robbing you. Actually, I'm going to give you a hundred yuan."

"Let me go." Skinny continued to struggle.

"Two hundred yuan."

"Let go of me."

"Three hundred yuan." Ma persisted.

"What do you want?" Skinny stopped struggling.

"I want an answer from you. Was it a trap when you talked me into going to the footbath?"

Skinny sized him up and said, "Give me the money first."

Ma took his wallet out of his backpack and counted out 300 yuan for Skinny, who put it in his pocket.

"You got us, Elder Brother. We're anglers."

"Are you in cahoots with the joint defense team?"

"How else would we catch a fish without working with them?" Skinny rolled his eyes at Ma. "They call it angling to enforce the law. We notified them the moment you walked in."

Ma nodded to show he understood. He had been caught visiting a prostitute not because of carelessness but because of a trap that others had set. Apparently, it was part of the game when Little Cui put a condom on him before starting her oral service; she needed the evidence for her partners to enforce the law. So, it was clearly a lie when she said she had canker sores. What a difference between a fine of 200–300 yuan for a prostitute and the 2,400 yuan they got out of their scheme. It's truly a lawless society when a train station joint defense team works with a pimp and prostitutes to carry out such outrageous crimes. Yet Ma could do nothing, like a mute unable to express his feeling after eating bitter fruit, because he did not know anyone in the city and, moreover, they still had the condom.

"What you've done is truly immoral," Ma said emotionally. "It's understandable that a man like you might do something this terrible, but the joint defense team is part of law enforcement, and they're clearly using their power to benefit themselves when they team up with you."

"They have to find creative ways for extra revenue." Skinny sneered. "Their superiors set goals for them. How could they get a monthly bonus if they weren't creative?"

"How do you split up the money?" Ma asked.

"We're paid as anglers, 100 yuan each, and they take the rest."

Ma did a quick calculation: 300 yuan for the three from the footbath, leaving 2,100 yuan for the joint defense team.

"It's peanuts. Why do you do it?"

"They're in charge of public security in this area. If we don't, we'll have to close up shop."

Ma stomped his foot in anger.

"This is rotten to the core."

"You may think you've lost money today, but actually you didn't lose anything." Skinny tried to make him feel better when he saw Ma's angry look.

"What do you mean?"

"Do you know who serviced you?"

"A woman in her fifties."

"Do you know her name?"

"Isn't she called Little Cui?"

"That's the name she uses at the bath. Her real name is Kang Shuping."

"Who's that?" Ma was baffled.

"Do you recall the case that rocked the country last year? A governor called Li Anbang got a life sentence for corruption? She's his wife."

Ma's head nearly exploded. He knew all about Li Anbang from the year before. As a government cadre, Ma was interested in scandals among high officials, but he had only been aware that Li got a life sentence. He never dreamed that he'd run into Li's wife and be serviced by her.

"Why, why is, she here?" Ma stammered.

"Her son also got a prison sentence over a traffic accident. He's serving it at a nearby juvenile correction center. It's too far from their hometown to travel back and forth, so she stays here for the monthly visit."

"She didn't have to become a prostitute to see her son, did she?"

"She's away from home and needs money for everything. Don't judge her."

"Still, can't she do something else?"

"Sure, she can. She can wash dishes for 2,000 yuan a month. But she isn't just visiting her son. Li Anbang was imprisoned in Qincheng, so she has to go to Beijing once a month to see him, too." Skinny continued, "Besides, she needs to grease the palms of those who can reduce her son's sentence or at least give him light work. All that requires money, and she can make it faster this way."

Ma nodded, but countered, despite his understanding of Kang Shuping's circumstances. "She shouldn't cheat people just because she needs the money."

"You wouldn't say that if you were in her shoes. I feel sorry for her. She's not young, so she gets few clients and makes little money. I've seen her weeping at night doing her accounts." Skinny added, "No one but us knows about it. I wouldn't have told you if you hadn't offered me money. You should be happy now that you've been serviced by the wife of a governor."

Skinny walked off, leaving a dazed Ma Zhongcheng behind. The human world can be so changeable. Ma shook his head. He had thought that Kang was vile to work in cahoots with the defense team, before he had known her identity, but now after learning her situation, he had a different view about her horrid acts. He had been stung by the injustice of the fine and its amount, before knowing her identity, but now the knowledge had him thinking that he had spent 2,400 yuan for oral service from a governor's wife. It was worth it. As the deputy chief of the environmental protection bureau, he would never get to meet a governor, let alone come into contact with a governor's wife. In a way, he could now consider himself having met a governor. Ma felt so much better now, knowing that he'd had a governor's wife, even though he would never get to meet a high official face-to-face. He would have done it with her, had he known she was Li Anbang's wife. It would be like eating a fish two ways. Then he recalled what the media had said about Li's downfall; it had something to do with a woman called Song Caixia, who was a prostitute herself. She had slept with Li, which turned out to be the key in Li's corruption case. Ma and Song were total strangers, but she might as well have lent him a hand in what had happened on this day. Her sleeping with Li had made a difference in Ma's dealing with Li's wife. For the first time, Ma realized what intricate connections draw total strangers together. Li Anbang and his son were the only two in the dark at the moment. Li would never know there was someone called Ma Zhongcheng, who had sneaked in from behind to have sex with his wife. Kang Shuping surely would not tell her son about her real job when she went to see him at the juvenile correction center, nor would she say a word about the footbath when she visited her husband in Qincheng Prison, thousands of li away. Then it occurred to Ma that he would not be the only man who had done that to Li. Who knows how many men had done the same, after she'd been working at the footbath and receiving clients daily for a long time? Song Caixia had not only "helped" Ma out, but she had done a good deal for many men. A cold sweat broke out on Ma's back as he thought about it, a dirty affair. He sighed as he glanced at his crotch. A major case that had shaken the whole country the year before had ended in a footbath, and a prostitute had turned a governor's wife into another one. The whole thing felt absurd, Ma thought. It was even more absurd when members of a joint defense team used prostitution to angle for money. What was so absurd about it? It was not absurd until some people made it part of their job, which, when he thought about it, was actually not that. What was truly absurd was how the joint defense team members took the scammed money home for their wives to spend on daily necessities. Everyone was doing something absurd, and everyone lived off the absurdity, which made it normal. But at the same time, it was how Ma himself had dodged the bullet on this day. If the defense team members had followed the rules, instead of angling for money, where would he be now? Likely in a detention center, on the road to ruination, reputation gone, family destroyed. So, he had the wives of the defense team members to thank for his escape from danger; they and their daily lives had provided a livelihood for Kang Shuping, and now a way out for Ma Zhongcheng, but in different ways, that is.

"What can I say?" Ma mused.

8

Ma Zhongcheng returned to the train station and sat back down on the flowerbed. He was lost in thought when his cell phone rang.

"Are you on the train?" It was his wife.

Roused from his reverie, Ma tried to compose himself.

"I just got a ticket. They were sold out because of the Labor Day golden week. Is everything all right?"

"I just got a call from my mother. Her lumbar disk hernia is acting up again, so take her to see a herbal doctor when you get home."

"All right."

"When you get back, make sure to sprinkle some food into the fish tank every day and don't forget to water the flowers. Can you remember all that?"

"All right."

He was glad the phone call had not come earlier; if it had, he would have still been with the defense team, and they would likely have taken the call. He would have been found out. He had escaped from another danger, despite the absurdity.

"Lucky me." Ma stuck his tongue out and said.

A heavyset man walked up.

"How about a footbath, Elder Brother? It'll make you feel good."

Ma shook his head.

"Our footbath isn't far. Just over there."

Ma shook his head again.

"Our girls are pretty."

Ma kept shaking his head.

"It's holiday time, Elder Brother. Can't I talk you into it?"

"You'll stop trying if I tell you this."

"What is it?"

"I run a footbath back home myself," Ma said.

"So, we're in the same business," the man paused before he burst out laughing. "I'll stop trying and wish you a safe journey home."

About the Author

Liu Zhenyun is one of China's best-known authors and screenwriters. By the mid-1980s, Liu began publishing short stories and novellas, many of which are now classics of contemporary literature, including *Tofu*; *College*; *Office*; *Officials*; *Recruits*; and *Remembering 1942*. Later novels, such as *Cellphone*; *The Cook, the Crook, and the Real Estate Tycoon*; *Nonsense Talk*; *Someone To Talk To*; *I Did Not Kill My Husband*; and *Strange Bedfellows* have become critically-acclaimed prize-winners as well as best-sellers among readers. His numerous awards include China's highest literary honor, the Mao Dun Literature Prize (2011), and France's Knight of the Order of Arts and Letters (2018). His works have been translated into a number of languages, including English, French, German, Italian, Spanish, Portuguese, Swedish, Dutch, Russian, Czech, Hungarian, Romanian, Serbian, Hebrew, Arabic, Turkish, Japanese, Korean, Vietnamese, and Thai. To date, over 15 million copies of Liu's works have been sold in China, and more of his fiction has been adapted for the screen than that of any other major Chinese author.

About the Translators

Howard Goldblatt is Emeritus Professor of East Asian Languages at the University of Colorado, subsequently Research Professor at the University of Notre Dame. A Guggenheim Fellow and founding editor of the journal *Modern Chinese Literature*, he has received honorary degrees from Hong Kong and British universities. Author or editor of more than a dozen books, in Chinese and English, he is the translator of more than fifty Chinese-language books, including ten by the 2012 Nobel Laureate Mo Yan, and two winners of the Asian Booker Prize. He has co-translated nearly two dozen works with Sylvia Li-chun Lin, one the winner of the Asian Booker, another the recipient of the Translation of the Year Award from the American Literary Translators Association. One of the most recent is *A Son of Taiwan*. He has also published a collection of flash fiction entitled *A Night in a Chinese Hospital*.

Sylvia Li-chun Lin, a native of Tainan, Taiwan, earned a doctoral degree in Comparative Literature from the University of California at Berkeley. She was Associate Professor of Chinese at the University of Notre Dame before resigning to become a full-time translator and writer. Author of *Representing Atrocity in Taiwan: The 2/28 Incident and White Terror in Fiction and Film*, she is professionally and personally invested in fictional works dealing with this part of Taiwan's past. She coedited *Documenting Taiwan on Film: Issues and Methods in New Documentaries* and *A Son of Taiwan*.

www.ingramcontent.com/pod-product-compliance
Lightning Source LLC
Chambersburg PA
CBHW020328240426
43665CB00044B/893